ING
VIEWPOINTS®
SERIES

Islam

WITHDRAWN
PRINT

Other Books of Related Interest:

Opposing Viewpoints Series
The Middle East

At Issue Series
How Should the U.S. Proceed in Afghanistan?

Current Controversies Series
Darfur

"Congress shall make no law . . . abridging the freedom of speech, or of the press."

First Amendment to the U.S. Constitution

The basic foundation of our democracy is the First Amendment guarantee of freedom of expression. The Opposing Viewpoints Series is dedicated to the concept of this basic freedom and the idea that it is more important to practice it than to enshrine it.

Islam

David M. Haugen, Susan Musser, and Kacy Lovelace,
Book Editors

GREENHAVEN PRESS
A part of Gale, Cengage Learning

Detroit • New York • San Francisco • New Haven, Conn • Waterville, Maine • London

Christine Nasso, *Publisher*
Elizabeth Des Chenes, *Managing Editor*

© 2009 Greenhaven Press, a part of Gale, Cengage Learning.

Gale and Greenhaven Press are registered trademarks used herein under license.

For more information, contact:
Greenhaven Press
27500 Drake Rd.
Farmington Hills, MI 48331-3535
Or you can visit our Internet site at gale.cengage.com

For product information and technology assistance, contact us at

Gale Customer Support, 1-800-877-4253
For permission to use material from this text or product, submit all requests online at
www.cengage.com/permissions

Further permissions questions can be emailed to permissionrequest@cengage.com

Articles in Greenhaven Press anthologies are often edited for length to meet page requirements. In addition, original titles of these works are changed to clearly present the main thesis and to explicitly indicate the author's opinion. Every effort is made to ensure that Greenhaven Press accurately reflects the original intent of the authors. Every effort has been made to trace the owners of copyrighted material.

Cover Image copyright Distinctive Images, 2009. Used under license from Shutterstock.com.

LIBRARY OF CONGRESS CATALOGING-IN-PUBLICATION DATA

Islam / David M. Haugen, Susan Musser, & Kacy Lovelace, book editors.
    p. cm. -- (Opposing viewpoints)
    Includes bibliographical references and index.
    ISBN 978-0-7377-4526-9 (hardcover)
    ISBN 978-0-7377-4527-6 (pbk.)
    1. Islam--Juvenile literature. I. Haugen, David M., 1969- II. Musser, Susan. III. Lovelace, Kacy.
    BP161.3.I722 2009
    297--dc22

                            2009014564

Printed in the United States of America
1 2 3 4 5 6 7 13 12 11 10 09

Contents

Why Consider Opposing Viewpoints?

> *"The only way in which a human being can make some approach to knowing the whole of a subject is by hearing what can be said about it by persons of every variety of opinion and studying all modes in which it can be looked at by every character of mind. No wise man ever acquired his wisdom in any mode but this."*
>
> John Stuart Mill

In our media-intensive culture it is not difficult to find differing opinions. Thousands of newspapers and magazines and dozens of radio and television talk shows resound with differing points of view. The difficulty lies in deciding which opinion to agree with and which "experts" seem the most credible. The more inundated we become with differing opinions and claims, the more essential it is to hone critical reading and thinking skills to evaluate these ideas. Opposing Viewpoints books address this problem directly by presenting stimulating debates that can be used to enhance and teach these skills. The varied opinions contained in each book examine many different aspects of a single issue. While examining these conveniently edited opposing views, readers can develop critical thinking skills such as the ability to compare and contrast authors' credibility, facts, argumentation styles, use of persuasive techniques, and other stylistic tools. In short, the Opposing Viewpoints Series is an ideal way to attain the higher-level thinking and reading skills so essential in a culture of diverse and contradictory opinions.

In addition to providing a tool for critical thinking, Opposing Viewpoints books challenge readers to question their own strongly held opinions and assumptions. Most people form their opinions on the basis of upbringing, peer pressure, and personal, cultural, or professional bias. By reading carefully balanced opposing views, readers must directly confront new ideas as well as the opinions of those with whom they disagree. This is not to simplistically argue that everyone who reads opposing views will—or should—change his or her opinion. Instead, the series enhances readers' understanding of their own views by encouraging confrontation with opposing ideas. Careful examination of others' views can lead to the readers' understanding of the logical inconsistencies in their own opinions, perspective on why they hold an opinion, and the consideration of the possibility that their opinion requires further evaluation.

Evaluating Other Opinions

To ensure that this type of examination occurs, Opposing Viewpoints books present all types of opinions. Prominent spokespeople on different sides of each issue as well as well-known professionals from many disciplines challenge the reader. An additional goal of the series is to provide a forum for other, less known, or even unpopular viewpoints. The opinion of an ordinary person who has had to make the decision to cut off life support from a terminally ill relative, for example, may be just as valuable and provide just as much insight as a medical ethicist's professional opinion. The editors have two additional purposes in including these less known views. One, the editors encourage readers to respect others' opinions—even when not enhanced by professional credibility. It is only by reading or listening to and objectively evaluating others' ideas that one can determine whether they are worthy of consideration. Two, the inclusion of such viewpoints encourages the important critical thinking skill of objectively evaluating an author's credentials and bias. This evaluation will illuminate an author's reasons for taking a particular stance on an issue and will aid in readers' evaluation of the author's ideas.

It is our hope that these books will give readers a deeper understanding of the issues debated and an appreciation of the complexity of even seemingly simple issues when good and honest people disagree. This awareness is particularly important in a democratic society such as ours in which people enter into public debate to determine the common good. Those with whom one disagrees should not be regarded as enemies but rather as people whose views deserve careful examination and may shed light on one's own.

Thomas Jefferson once said that "difference of opinion leads to inquiry, and inquiry to truth." Jefferson, a broadly educated man, argued that "if a nation expects to be ignorant and free . . . it expects what never was and never will be." As individuals and as a nation, it is imperative that we consider the opinions of others and examine them with skill and discernment. The Opposing Viewpoints Series is intended to help readers achieve this goal.

David L. Bender and Bruno Leone,
Founders

Introduction

"*I'm very happy that most Muslims are willing to live in peace with their neighbors. Yet we have to be honest here. Benevolent Muslims aren't peaceful because they are following the example set by Muhammad. They are peaceful because they've chosen to do what's right, and because they are willing to live far better lives than Muhammad himself lived.*"

David Wood,
"The Two Faces of
Islam . . . Still Smiling,"
Answering Islam.
www.answering-islam.org.

Since the terrorist attacks of September 11, 2001, many in the Western world have painted Islam as a religion and an ideology of aggression—one that stands in stark contrast to the peaceful, democratic principles that supposedly embody Western liberal thought. However, as the war against terrorism has dragged on and radical elements of the Islamic world have gained larger followings, Western leaders have recognized that containing Muslim extremism cannot be accomplished without reaching out to the masses of moderate Muslims both in the East and in the West.

At a speech given in 2007 at the rededication of the Islamic Center in Washington, D.C., President George W. Bush stated, "The greatest challenge facing people of conscience is to help the forces of moderation win the great struggle against extremism that is now playing out across the broader Middle East." In making a distinction between moderates and radicals, the president said of Muslim extremists, "This self-appointed vanguard presumes to speak for Muslims. They do not. They call all Muslims who do not believe in their harsh and hateful ideology 'infidels' and 'betrayers' of the true Muslim faith. This enemy falsely claims that America is at war with Muslims and the Muslim faith, when in fact it is these radicals who are Islam's true enemy."

President Bush's words were carefully chosen to reinforce the administration's claim that there is a rift in Islam between the majority of mainstream, peaceful Muslim adherents and a minority of violent fundamentalists who are shielding their heinous acts behind the banner of their faith. Suggesting this division is an important strategy in the war against terrorism, for as Radwan Masmoudi, president of the Center for the Study of Islam & Democracy in Washington, D.C., has made clear, "To defeat the terrorists, the United States must avoid even the appearance that this is a war against Islam." Masmoudi stipulates the United States can only win its struggle by "reaching out to moderate Muslim leaders everywhere, establishing trust, engaging them in a dialogue, and understanding their issues and concerns" and by "supporting moderate Muslim leaders (both religious and secular) who are calling for a modern, tolerant, peaceful, and democratic interpretation of Islam."

Not everyone, however, is convinced reaching out to moderate Muslims—whom supporters claim represent the vast majority of the world's 1.5 billion Muslims—is the right strategy to win the war against terrorism, build democracy, and bring about peace. Indeed, some have pointed out that dialoguing with moderate factions has done little to change the growth of fundamentalism or curb radicalism in Islamic nations. Ronald R. Krebs, an assistant professor of political science at the University of Minnesota, argued in a 2008 edition of the online news source *Slate* that the problem with the strategy is moderate Muslims have no unique voice or alternative ideology to offer would-be radical converts. He claims,

"Muslim moderates cannot be mobilized until they exist as a legitimate political force with an agenda distinct from that of their extremist co-religionists." And in Krebs's view, this political force must be a true alternative for young and unaffiliated Muslims, offering "an ambivalent political posture that distances them both from more extreme Islamists and from true-believing Westernizers." Krebs still advocates U.S. support for moderate Muslim groups, but he attests that if these organizations show any connection to the West, they will fail in drawing potential extremists away from the radical fold.

Robert Spencer, the director of Jihad Watch, a blog that follows the spreading influence of Islam and its militant ideology, simply disagrees that moderate Muslims exist as a separate entity in Islam. According to Spencer, "'Moderate Islam' as a viable entity is still in an inchoate state theologically; it is largely a cultural habit that is ever vulnerable to being overturned by by-the-book radicals." Because of this, Spencer adds, "It is not so easy to find Muslim leaders who have genuinely renounced violent jihad and any intention, now or in the future, to impose Sharia [strict Muslim law] on non-Muslim countries." Spencer points out in a 2004 article posted on Jihad Watch that some of the so-called moderate Muslims who are living in the United States and courted by the U.S. government have espoused some anti–U.S. rhetoric on a number of occasions.

Politically incorrect speech aside, moderate Muslims may be more of a silent majority than closeted extremists, as Spencer argues. In his definition of moderate Muslims, Muqtedar Khan, an associate professor of political science at the University of Delaware, states moderate Muslims shun this nomenclature because it implies they have sold out their faith for Western ideals. Instead, he contends moderates are generally "reflective, self-critical, pro-democracy and human-rights and closet secularists." As Khan claims, moderate Muslims are not interested in freeing territory through jihad but rather in freeing minds through enlightened understanding of Islamic faith. "Moderate Muslims aspire for a society—a city of virtue—that will treat all people with dignity and respect. There will be no room for political or normative intimidation," Khan maintains.

Angel Rabasa, a senior policy analyst at the Rand Corporation [a nonprofit, nonpartisan think tank], concurs that moderate Muslims make up the majority of Islam's followers but lack the voice and presence of radical factions. Rabasa suggests this is because extremists have better developed networks to spread their ideologies. He states, "Liberal and moderate Muslims, although a majority in almost all countries, have not created similar networks. Muslim moderates feel exposed and isolated. Their voices are often fractured or silenced."

Whether Western leaders will ever be able to reach out to moderate Muslims and whether these moderates will find a collective voice to respond is uncertain in an era still marked by the politically and culturally divisive war against terrorism and military operations in Iraq and Afghanistan. But as President Bush assured the silent majority of moderate Muslims yearning for peace and liberty from radical tyranny, "You plead in silence no longer. The free world hears you. You are not alone."

In *Opposing Viewpoints: Islam*, the voices of some moderate Muslims are heard. In chapters such as Are the Values of Islam and the West in Conflict? Does Islam Promote Violence? What Is the Status of Women Under Islam? and What Is the Future of Islam? Islamic and Western experts and writers debate various issues relating to Islam and its impact on world affairs. Some of these commentators portray Islam as more of a political ideology than a religion—one that insists its faith is superior and will not abide nonbelievers. Others are moderates who believe Islam is a peaceful religion—one of many faiths coexisting on the planet. Collectively, these speakers and authors explicitly or implicitly acknowledge that for there to be peace between East and West, Muslims must address the divisions that exist between moderates and extremists in Islam.

OPPOSING
VIEWPOINTS®
SERIES

CHAPTER 1

Are the Values of Islam and the West in Conflict?

Chapter Preface

In 2005, David Blankenhorn, the founder and president of the Institute for American Values, spoke to an assembly of Muslim clerics and leaders in Muscat, Oman. Hoping to encourage dialogue between Islam and Christianity and promote shared interests in a post–September 11, 2001, world, Blankenhorn told the gathering, "We are two very different societies, of course, each with its own distinctive traditions and gifts, but we also have much in common." To elucidate his claim, he drew parallels between Muslim and Christian scripture before listing what he argued are some of the universal values all people of "good will" share:

> The idea that all persons are created equal. The idea that moral truths exist and are accessible to all people. The idea that our understanding of the truth is always imperfect, so that most disagreements about values call for civility, openness to other views, and reasonable argument in pursuit of truth. And finally, the importance of freedom of conscience and freedom of religion.

Blankenhorn anticipated such shared values could help defuse the tensions arising from a presumed ideological struggle between East and West. Ultimately, Blankenhorn looked forward to a partnership in which Muslims and Christians would "replace the clash of civilizations with a global civil society guided by universal human values and based on the principles of justice and tolerance."

Some critics, however, believe such a utopian partnership is impossible. Photojournalist and radio talk show host Lan Lamphere argues Islam is not a tolerant religion and seeks only to convert nonbelievers or destroy them. Building on the definition of Islam as "submission to the will of God," Lamphere insists "Islam demands submission from the whole world." In an article for his Town Hall Internet blog, he states

Islam is not content with the live-and-let-live philosophy adopted and practiced by the Westernized people of Europe and the United States. Instead, Islam, in his view, "exist[s] in a constant state of ultimatums" that require non-Muslims to either submit or perish. Such an intractable philosophy, Lamphere and others believe, could never lead to compromise or the union of spirit that those such as Blankenhorn envision. In fact, Lamphere maintains Muslims view Western tolerance as a weakness to be exploited in a global contest for religious domination.

In the following chapter, various authors examine the compatibility of Western and Islamic values. Some see shared ideals as a bridge to further compassion and understanding. Others contend a clash of civilizations is inevitable because Islam supposedly divides the world rigidly into believers and infidels.

"The quest for democracy among Muslims today is one of the most prominent and transformative features of our time."

An Islamic Democracy Can Exist

Anwar Ibrahim

The desire to be free and live in a democratic society is not unique to the West, argues Anwar Ibrahim in the viewpoint that follows. Ibrahim contends the religion of Islam promotes many of the core values of democracy such as "freedom of conscience, freedom of expression, and the sanctity of life and property." While admitting there is still work to be done to establish democracies throughout the Muslim world, he cites examples of successful modern Muslim democracies. Ibrahim is a politician from Malaysia who was deputy prime minister of that country from 1993 to 1998.

As you read, consider the following questions:

1. What are some of the principles Ibrahim claims are valued by both democracy and Islam?

Anwar Ibrahim, "Universal Values and Muslim Democracy," *Journal of Democracy*, vol. 17, July 2006, pp. 5–12. Copyright © 2006 National Endowment for Democracy and The Johns Hopkins University Press. Reproduced by permission.

2. What are two Muslim countries that have successfully implemented democratic governments, according to the author?

3. What does the author argue must be done for Muslim democracies to progress and flourish worldwide?

At this pivotal moment in history, when East and West are growing increasingly alienated from one another over issues of freedom and justice, I am reminded of our upbringing in multicultural and multiethnic Malaysia. It was this upbringing that infused the Malaysian psyche with what Nobel laureate Amartya Sen has described as a plurality of identities. By nature we Malaysians are an inquisitive people, interested in other faiths and cultures. We studied the Koran and the traditions of the Prophet Muhammad at the same time that we devoured the works of [Alighieri] Dante [thirteenth- and fourteenth-century Florentine poet whose most famous work is the *Divine Comedy*], Shakespeare, and T.S. Eliot [poet, playwright, and literary critic who was born in the United States in 1888 and later moved to England, where he died in 1965]. For me, there has never been any doubt that our world and the West are compatible, and that this spirit of inclusiveness and pluralism will continue to be a source of inspiration in bridging the gaps between cultures and civilizations.

Yet there are some who persist in arguing vehemently that the great civilizations are destined for confrontation if not outright conflict. While the end of the Cold War gave a great boost to the spread of freedom and gave rise to a prevailing sense of optimism, in many corners of the earth these values have yet to take root. On the contrary, we see fundamental liberties being trampled upon and abused, fueling discord among nations and civilizations. My own struggle against those who seek to keep humanity shrouded in tyranny led to my incarceration [in Malaysia on charges of corruption and sodomy] for six years, a time during which I realized with blinding clarity that freedom is the very essence of being which unlocks the full potential of the human spirit.

There are many who believe that democracy is a construct of the West, molded in response to the peculiar historical circumstances that shaped it. Others argue that freedom and democracy, while suitable in some parts of the world, are by no means universal goods. They say that other nations ought not to adopt the ways of freedom and democracy without due regard to their own political, cultural, and social traditions.

Successful Democracies Exist Outside the West

It is true that the founding principles of constitutional democracy, as we know it today, have their antecedents in the political philosophy of [English philosopher] John Locke, which through the writings of Voltaire [French philosopher whose real name was François-Marie Arouet] entered France and then deeply influenced the framers of the U.S. Constitution. But the fact that these principles of political freedom and democracy were first articulated in the West does not preclude them from universal application, nor can it be asserted that they have not been expressed in other contexts.

It has been argued, for example, that "Asian values" developed in clear opposition to democratic values. Confucian ethics [established by Chinese philosopher Confucius in the sixth and fifth centuries B.C.E.] is cited in this respect as stressing the importance of filial piety, and, by extension, submission to state authority. But this argument completely ignores another central precept of Confucian ethics, which, as [contemporary Chinese philosopher and Confucianist] Tu Wei-Ming correctly asserts, also emphasizes the primacy of the self and the importance of self-cultivation in realizing human potential and guarding against exploitation by the powers that be.

Amartya Sen and another Nobel laureate, former South Korean president Kim Dae Jung, have effectively debunked the

Asian-values thesis. The experiences of South Korea and Taiwan, two states with a clearly Confucian ethical heritage, further lay waste to the notion that Western concepts of democracy are incompatible with Asian civilization. Thailand, a state with a largely Buddhist population, and Indonesia, with the largest Muslim population in the world, have also succeeded in building democracies. Contrasted with these examples, the false discourse of "Asian values" merely shows how far authoritarian rulers, along with their cronies and apologists, will go in order to justify and preserve their rule. Although autocrats remain entrenched in some places, their influence over the masses is waning, and it is undeniable that Asian peoples have demonstrated not only their desire to promote democratic principles, but also their ability to sustain democratic institutions and freedoms.

Roots of Democracy Are in Islam

Harrowing theories have also been concocted claiming an inherent contradiction between Islam and democratic values, in an attempt to drive a wedge between two great civilizations. It is said, for example, that whereas liberal democracy places sovereignty in the hands of the individual, in Islam sovereignty belongs solely to God, thereby reducing the individual to a mere agent with little concern for the exercise of creativity and personal freedom. This view is a misreading of the sources of religion and represents a capitulation to extremist discourse. The proper view is that freedom is the fundamental objective of the divine law. Islam has always expressed the primacy of *'adl*, or justice, which is a close approximation of what the West defines as freedom. Justice entails ruling according to the dictates of Islamic law, which emphasize consultation and condemn despotism and tyranny.

As articulated by the great jurist [Imam] al-Shatibi (d. 790 C.E.), the *maqasid al-shari'a* (higher objectives of the *shari'a* [Islamic law]) sanctify the preservation of religion, life, intellect, family, and wealth, objectives that bear striking resemblance to Lockean [based on John Locke's] ideals that would be expounded centuries later. Many scholars have further explained that laws which contravene the *maqasid* must be revised or amended to bring them into line with the higher objectives and to ensure that they contribute to the safety and development of the individual and society. Notwithstanding the current malaise of authoritarianism plaguing the Muslim world, there can be no question that several crucial elements of constitutional democracy and civil society are also moral imperatives in Islam—freedom of conscience, freedom of expression, and the sanctity of life and property—as demonstrated very clearly by the Koran, as well as by the teachings of the Prophet Muhammad, perhaps most succinctly and eloquently in his farewell address.

There is an ongoing debate over these issues in the Muslim world. The extremist view, by conflating the exercise of state power with the sovereignty of God, confers on tyranny the mantle of legitimacy. On the other hand, the secular elite espouses a vision that purports to eliminate the role of religion within the public sphere. The current assertions about Islam's hostility to democracy hold no more water than did the discredited Asian-values thesis.

The World's Largest Muslim-Majority Democracy

The quest for democracy among Muslims today is one of the most prominent and transformative features of our time. An earlier democratic wave brought down the Berlin Wall, liberated Eastern Europe from communism, and triggered the implosion of the Soviet Empire. Almost a decade later, Indonesia, the largest Muslim country in the world, broke free from the yoke of military-based authoritarian rule and plunged headlong into democracy after more than thirty years of oppression and dictatorship. Indonesia is the world's largest

Contractual and Consensual Rule in Islam

The traditional system of Islamic government is both consensual and contractual. The manuals of holy law generally assert that the new caliph—the head of the Islamic community and state—is to be "chosen." The Arabic term used is sometimes translated as "elected," but it does not connote a general or even sectional election. Rather, it refers to a small group of suitable, competent people choosing the ruler's successor. In principle, hereditary succession is rejected by the juristic tradition. Yet in practice, succession was always hereditary, except when broken by insurrection or civil war; it was—and in most places still is—common for a ruler, royal or otherwise, to designate his successor.

But the element of consent is still important. In theory, at times even in practice, the ruler's power—both gaining it and maintaining it—depends on the consent of the ruled. The basis of the ruler's authority is described in the classical texts by the Arabic word bay'a, a term usually translated as "homage," as in the subjects paying homage to their new ruler. But a more accurate translation of bay'a—which comes from a verb meaning "to buy and to sell"—would be "deal," in other words, a contract between the ruler and the ruled in which both have obligations.

Bernard Lewis,
"Freedom and Justice in the Modern Middle East,"
Foreign Affairs, *May/June 2005.*

Muslim-majority nation; its successful transition is the single most significant development in the recent history of democracy. The press in Indonesia is free, and the fairness of Indonesian elections is unsurpassed. Fundamental liberties are enshrined in the constitution and fully recognized and respected by the powers that be. The people may gather to protest government decisions and policies without fear of reprisal.

Still, efforts to bolster democratic institutions must be pursued relentlessly. Economic progress through free-market reforms must remain high on the list of priorities, with a concomitant program for socioeconomic justice. The fight against corruption must continue with full conviction. It is true that Indonesia still has significant steps to take, particularly toward fulfilling the socioeconomic objectives of democracy, but it undoubtedly remains a beacon for Muslim nations aspiring to attain democracy and freedom.

The Turkish Democracy Shows Progress and Promise

What happened in Indonesia in 1997 stands as one of the decisive moments in Islam's modern history. What is happening in Turkey in the current decade is no less remarkable. If Indonesia enjoys the prestige of being the largest Muslim country, Turkey is remembered among Muslims as the seat of their last great empire, as well as of the caliphate [a government that rules by Islamic law]. The Turkish Republic came into being after the First World War as a modern state with an avowedly secular character under Mustafa Kemal [founder and first president of the Republic of Turkey]. Until recently, however, Turkish democracy was beset by a fundamental contradiction: Its secular character was maintained not by popular consent, but by military force. Moreover, secularism had morphed into a religion of its own. Hopes of joining the European Union have helped to contain the once unrestricted power of the military elite and to open up political space in which parties may operate without fear of reprisal. In this new climate, the current government has a clear democratic mandate from the people. The work that Turkey has done in order to navigate its way to a "new consensus" marks the country as one of the most vibrant and mature Muslim democracies. It is within a democratic framework that this nation aspires to refresh its collective memory of its cultural heritage. Turkey seeks to mature further as a democracy while retaining its Muslim identity.

Turkish prime minister Recep Tayyip Erdogan, the former "people's mayor" of Istanbul who spent time in jail for his devotion to his political convictions, embodies the qualities needed to advance democratic reforms and social justice. Under his leadership, secularism is no longer seen as "against religion" but rather as a fundamental principle of impartiality and tolerance of religious diversity. To my mind, if a modern democratic Muslim state seeks to set limits on governmental authority in deference to the rights of the individual, this is wholly in line with the requirements of constitutional democracy.

Though the relevance of the Turkish experience to the rest of the Muslim world may seem self-evident, there is considerable dispute over the lessons to be drawn from it. According to some interpretations, for example, the primary lesson of the Turkish case is that a secular political order is a prerequisite for constitutional democracy. But the experiences of Egypt and Iraq under Nasserism and Baathism, respectively, clearly reveal that secularism, far from being a guarantee of constitutional democracy, may become a formula for tyranny. Indonesia under Suharto [authoritarian president of Indonesia from 1967 to 1998] was explicitly secular, but it certainly was not a constitutional democracy. It is more correct to say that constitutional democracy cannot take root in a society, whether secular or Islamic, without a firm and profound commitment on the part of the political elites to protect the fundamental rights of all. . . .

The Innate Desire for Freedom

For many of us, the debate about democratization is anything but theoretical. It emanates from our innate desire for honor and dignity and the natural human instinct for survival and development. Every day that passes without change means another bleak night for political prisoners languishing in solitude, another death from hunger and disease as a result of neglect and deprivation, and another opportunity for the corrupt to abscond with millions from state coffers.

This debate is about the people's compact with the state, about governance and accountability. We reject the arrogance of power, the machinations of the intelligence apparatus, and the suspension of civil liberties, be it in mature or emerging democracies. We should not apply double standards, condemning Saddam Hussein as the perpetrator of crimes against humanity and turning a blind eye to the current atrocities in Iraq. While we condemn the inhuman treatment of prisoners at Abu Ghraib, we must not ignore the deplorable treatment of political prisoners across the Muslim world. We will not be successful in the struggle for democratic reform unless we are optimistic and have trust in the wisdom of the people.

Continuing the Fight for Democracy Reform

The future of Muslim democracy is now. The emergence of Muslim democracies is something significant and worthy of our attention. Yet with the clear exceptions of Indonesia and Turkey, the Muslim world today is a place where autocracies and dictatorships of various shades and degrees continue their parasitic hold on the people, gnawing away at their newfound freedoms. While it is true that some positive changes are in evidence in the Middle East, it must be stressed that we are still a long way from realizing our cherished ideals of freedom and democracy, ideals that we find in the Islamic intellectual tradition, where unjust and corrupt leaders are held to account—a tradition illustrated by the allegorical tales found in the twelfth-century *Sulwan* (a guidebook for just rulers) of [twelfth-century, Arab philosopher and political activist, Ibn] Zafar al-Siqilli.

If democracy is about nurturing a "spirit of dissent," then it has indeed been part and parcel of Muslim cultural history, founded on a tradition attributed to the Prophet Muhammad that the divergence of opinions among scholars is a *rahmah* (blessing). The great founding jurists of the major schools of law in Islam adamantly protested against their own school being adopted as the state canon of their time. Many were imprisoned as a result. We are the inheritors of this tradition, which provides today's Muslims with a storehouse of democratic ideas. But as T.S. Eliot reminds us, between the idea and the reality falls the shadow.

The light that will make this shadow vanish is engagement, to be pursued relentlessly with courage and conviction. We must reject the marginalization of people merely because of their political convictions. We must ensure that democratic institutions are firmly in place to accommodate a broad spectrum of political perspectives, modern or traditional, liberal or Islamist. The West must not view the traditional scholars as being against freedom or democracy. Many have been fighting for freedom and justice, and many have paid a high price for it. It is a mistake to engage only with the liberals while ignoring the leaders who command the support of the majority. Our challenge will be to engage with the broadest spectrum, without compromising our commitment to freedom and democracy.

The conclusion we must draw from these legacies is that the human desire to be free and to lead a dignified life is universal. So is the abhorrence of despotism and oppression. These are passions that motivate not only Muslims but people from all civilizations.

> *"Dictatorship, poverty, brutality, and backwardness are the norm across the Muslim world, and Islam is systemically designed to keep the situation this way."*

An Islamic Democracy Cannot Exist

Anonymous

In the viewpoint that follows, the author claims democracy-building in Iraq and other Islamic countries cannot be a short-term goal of U.S. foreign policy. In the author's view, democracy is a process that takes centuries and can thrive only where certain preconditions—such as a respect for the rule of law—exist. The author maintains that Islamic nations do not share the traditions necessary to convert to democracy so easily. However, the author insists it is still worth the effort to spread Western ideals in Muslim nations in hopes that over time some change can be made.

As you read, consider the following questions:

1. What are the three prerequisites the author states are necessary for democracy to take hold in a nation?

Anonymous, "The Mirage of Islamic Democracy," gatesofvienna.blogspot.com, December 11, 2007. Reproduced by permission. The original article can be found at http://gatesofvienna.blogspot.com/2007/12/mirage-of-islamic-democracy.html.

2. Why does the author believe tribal ruling structures are the norm throughout the Islamic world?

3. In the author's view, what has been responsible for keeping Islam on "artificial life-support" since the 1930s?

I just finished reading a series of articles about Iraq in various conservative magazines, and the good news is undeniable: the Surge [the 2007 deployment of more than 20,000 additional U.S. troops to Iraq] is working. Al Qaeda has been routed in the last six months or so [of 2007], and the Sunni tribes which had been implacably hostile to the United States have now turned around and allied with us in their own self-interest.

An inescapable conclusion about the recent success is that it had nothing to do with Iraqi democracy. One hopes for the success of democracy in Iraq, but it was not democracy that brought down Al Qaeda in Iraq. In fact, it wasn't even good government that did the job. Chaos, corruption, and gridlock are still the order of the day within the Iraqi government.

What brought success in Iraq was recognizing and building on the existing tribal structures.

The Sunni tribes have no love for the "foreigners" in Al Qaeda, who bring violence, intimidation, and a challenge to their traditional ways. Realizing this, the U.S. military did the smart thing: it worked hard at undurstanding these tribal systems, and partnered with them to uphold their time-honored customs and defeat the interlopers. *That* was what succeeded against the "insurgency".

There Will Be No Democracy in Iraq

Needless to say, this was a quintessentially conservative strategy. But its success had nothing to do with democracy. In fact, insisting on a working democracy would almost certainly have guaranteed our failure.

This is a hard lesson to learn. However much a people yearns to be free, the removal of a tyrant does not guarantee the emergence of a peaceful liberal democracy.

Whenever the United States pulls out of Iraq, the best we can hope for is to leave behind a stable authoritarian government that is only *moderately* repressive and brutal towards its own people.

The dream is over.

What Is Needed for Democracy

America is famous for its short attention span. We want to get in, get the job done, and then get out and go back home to watch TV. With this kind of mindset, it's hard to look at the big picture, which may be a panorama that spans decades or centuries.

Unfortunately for us, the formation of a working democracy *is* a process that takes centuries.

First of all, there must be a long tradition of the rule of law. If a people has no experience of law except when enforced by the sword of a tyrant, then democracy is unlikely to develop. Organizing an election and persuading people to vote does not create a democracy. In order for the democratic process to succeed, the populace must already trust and respect an order which transcends the whim of the current thug in power.

The [people who founded the] United States had experienced centuries of the rule of law—that is, the well-defined and constitutionally limited powers of the King of England and the Parliament—before it could successfully form a constitutional republic.

Another required condition for democracy to flourish is civil society, a plurality of legally recognized and independent institutions. People who are used to governing themselves within smaller bodies—churches, civic organizations, commercial associations, sporting clubs, etc.—will find it relatively easy to extend the same principles to the entire polity.

The United States had experienced centuries of civil society—the guilds, local councils, universities, etc., in England, supplemented by religious pluralism and well-regulated militias within the colonies—before it could successfully form a constitutional republic.

The Populace Must Be Educated

A third prerequisite for democracy is the availability of a good general education. Not all of the populace has to be educated—the United States and various European democracies were founded by and flourished with a relatively small educated class—but the pool of potential rulers and legislators must be well-educated if the mechanics of democratic government are to be implemented effectively.

The United States had experienced several generations of successfully educating the sons of the landowners and the merchant class before it could successfully form a constitutional republic.

Unfortunately, none of these necessary prerequisites listed above is present in Iraq, or indeed in any Muslim country. With the partial exception of Turkey, for centuries the Islamic countries have known nothing but the rule of the strongman, a unitary society under Islam, and massive illiteracy. The conditions in which democracy might flourish simply do not exist.

Midwifing a democracy in Germany under Allied occupation after World War Two was possible because the necessary prerequisites had existed for centuries in Europe. Expecting the same thing in Iraq is futile. We can maintain a semblance of "democracy" as long as American troops are present, but after they leave the country will inevitably revert to what it has always known.

To create something different, we would have to do what the British did in India: control the civil administration in the country, enforce the use of our own language, and make success for the local administrators dependent upon abiding by our own rules—*and we would have to do it for more than two hundred years.*

Even if we did have imperial ambitions, we Americans would be unable to wait that long. So, sooner or later, we will get out of Iraq and call what we leave behind "democracy." After that Iraq will return to something more or less familiar.

It's like chopping down all the trees in the woods and then scattering a few seeds among the stumps. Why are we inevitably surprised when the resulting garden contains nothing but second-growth pines and weeds?

Democracy Does Not Flourish Under Islam

This is not to say that promoting democracy is a bad idea. Since we are much less likely to be threatened by a democracy than we are by a brutal tyranny, a prudent foreign policy requires that we encourage the emergence of democracies.

But first the necessary conditions for democracy must exist. Since we are unwilling to go the imperial route and force democracy down the throats of our unwilling subjects, what other course might we take?

The first step in solving the problem would be to acknowledge the elephant in the room: democracy does not flourish under Islam. The wishful thinking of George W. Bush does not change this unfortunate fact. Islam is an *obstacle* to democracy.

The U.S. military successfully co-opted the tribal culture to defeat Al Qaeda in Iraq, but that tribal culture, is not conducive to the development of democracy. The traditional tribal systems in the Middle East can function effectively under a strongman, a regional Sheikh [Arab leader or elder] constrained by the local tribal traditions. This is the best we can hope for under current conditions.

And it's important to realize that these conditions are maintained in stasis by Islam. The tenets of Islamic law do not allow for the development of anything else. The reason why atavistic tribal structures are the norm throughout the Islamic world is that the words of the Prophet have artificially preserved into the third millennium the social and political structures of antiquity.

It is illegal and blasphemous under Islam to construct a society based on the rule of law.

It is illegal and blasphemous under Islam to create the plural institutions necessary for a civil society.

It is illegal and blasphemous under Islam to educate men in non-Koranic subjects and to educate women at all.

Islam Is Declining

Without a systematic and concerted long-term effort to counter Islam directly, any attempt to promote democracy in Muslim countries is unlikely to succeed. Our goals should include undermining the attraction of Islamic ideas by highlighting and distributing alternative information. Much of Western culture is disturbing and repellent to the Muslim world, but—as is often the case with such things—much of it is also very attractive.

We *can* be successful, provided that we are unabashed in pursuit of our goal. Islam has been on artificial life-support for the last seventy years thanks to petroleum. It would have withered away by now had it not been for that little gift from Allah.

If it weren't for the petrodollars, one little push would bring the whole tottering edifice crashing down.

Dictatorship, poverty, brutality, and backwardness are the norm across the Muslim world, and Islam is systemically designed to keep the situation this way. Despotism and violence

Under Islam, the Laws Are Fixed Forever

Democracy means the rule of the demos, the common people, or what is now known as popular or national sovereignty. In Islam, however, power belongs only to God: al-hukm l'illah. The man who exercises that power on Earth is known as Khalifat al-Allah, the regent of God. Even then the Khalifah, or Caliph, cannot act as legislator. The law has already been spelt out and fixed forever by God.

The only task that remains is its discovery, interpretation and application. That, of course, allows for a substantial space in which different styles of rule could develop.

But the bottom line is that no Islamic government can be democratic in the sense of allowing the common people equal shares in legislation. Islam divides human activities into five categories from the permitted to the sinful, leaving little room for human interpretation, let alone ethical innovations.

Amir Taheri, "Islam and Democracy: The Impossible Union,"
Sunday Times (United Kingdom), May 23, 2004.

are the order of the day from Algeria and Libya across Egypt and the Arabian peninsula, branching off in one direction across South Asia and India to the archipelagos of the Indian Ocean, and into equatorial Africa in the other.

How likely is it that democracy will emerge in these places?

Containment Is the First Order

The opposite is much more likely; namely, that the gradual Islamization of Europe and other parts of the West will erode the existing Western democracies. If we mount no resistance to it, an imperceptible but steady reduction of liberty will prepare our people for the inevitable merger of the Islamic method of governance with our own. Eventually the term "democracy" will become an empty tool of the propagandists, with no more meaning than the word "republic" in the People's Republic of China.

A cold-eyed empirical evaluation points towards the containment, isolation, and quarantine of the existing Islamic states.

Only after that will a focus on democratization become a luxury that we can afford.

> *"As a religion founded by a business-man . . . and one that has cherished trade from its very beginning, Islam can in fact be very compatible with a capitalist economy."*

Islam Is Compatible with Capitalism

Mustafa Akyol

There is no inherent quality of Islam that makes it incompatible with capitalism, argues Mustafa Akyol in the following view-point. Akyol explores the historical embrace of capitalist prin-ciples—such as trade and profit-making—by the religion of Is-lam and its founding prophet Mohammed. In addition, he presents the capitalist system of Turkey as an example of what could be possible across the wider Islamic world if Islamic funda-mentalists would cease their opposition to capitalism on the basis of its Western roots. Akyol is a Turkish Muslim journalist living in Istanbul, Turkey, and has contributed to many Turkish and American publications.

As you read, consider the following questions:

1. According to the author, does the pretext for socialism exist in the Koran?

Mustafa Akyol, "Is Capitalism Compatible with Islam?" *Turkish Daily News*, February 19, 2007. Reproduced by permission.

2. What does the author identify as the one "bone of contention" that serves as a hurdle for the adoption of Islamic capitalism?

3. What distinction does the author believe is important to highlight to convince Muslims that capitalism is a valid economic system, compatible with Islamic beliefs?

Is Islam compatible with modernity? This has become a hotly debated question in the past few decades. Much of the discussion focuses on issues relating to political liberalism—democracy, pluralism and freedom of thought. Another important dimension of modernity is, of course, economic liberalism. So we should also ask whether Islam is compatible with it, i.e., a free-market economy, or capitalism.

Most Islamists would reply to this question with a resounding "No!" Since they perceive Islam as an all-encompassing socio-political system, they regard capitalism as a rival and an enemy. The struggle against both communism and capitalism has been one of the standard themes in Islamist literature. Sayyid Qutb, the prominent ideologue of the Egyptian Muslim Brotherhood, wrote a book titled *Ma'arakat al-Islam wa'l-Ra's Maliyya* (*The Battle Between Islam and Capitalism*) in 1951. At an Islamic conference held in the Spanish city of Granada in July 2003, attended by about 2,000 Muslims, a call was made to "bring about the end of the capitalist system."

However, such radical rejections of the capitalist economy don't seem well suited to the theological attitude and the historical experience of Islam towards business and profit making. As a religion founded by a businessman—the Prophet Mohammed was a successful merchant for the greater part of his life—and one that has cherished trade from its very beginning, Islam can in fact be very compatible with a capitalist economy supplemented by a set of moral values that emphasize the care of the poor and the needy.

An Openness to Business and Profit in the Koran

This interesting compatibility between Islam and capitalism has been studied extensively. A classic work on this theme is Maxime Rodinson's famed book, *Islam and Capitalism* (1966). Rodinson, a French Marxist, by appealing to the textual analysis of Islamic sources and the economic history of the Islamic world, demonstrated that Muslims had never had any trouble with making money. "There are religions whose sacred texts discourage economic activity in general," said Rodinson. "[However] this is certainly not the case with the Koran, which looks with favor upon commercial activity, confining itself to condemning fraudulent practices and requiring abstention from trade during certain religious festivals."

It is true that the Koran has a strong emphasis on social justice, and this has led some modern Muslim intellectuals to sympathize with socialism and its promise of a "classless society." A careful reading of the Koran would work against such "Islamo-socialism." The Muslim Scripture takes it as a given that there will be rich and poor people in society and, in a sense, ensures the disparity by actively supporting the rights to private property and inheritance. However, it persistently warns the well-off to care for the deprived. Zakat is the institutionalized form of this compassion: Every rich Muslim is obliged to give a certain amount of his wealth to his poor brethren.

Zakat is a voluntary act of charity, not a collectivization of wealth by a central authority. According to scholars John Thomas Cummings, Hossein Askari and Ahmad Mustafa,— who co-authored the academic paper, "Islam and Modern Economic Change"—"Zakat is primarily a voluntary act of piety and a far cry from what most modern-day taxpayers experience when confronted with increased income levies or complicated regulations." Moreover, they add, "there is no particular Islamic preference for [a] Marxist emphasis on economic planning over market forces."

Indeed, when the Prophet Mohammed was asked to fix the prices in the market because some merchants were selling goods too dearly, he refused and said, "Only Allah governs the market." It wouldn't be far-fetched to see a parallel here with [eighteenth-century Scottish philosopher who wrote *The Wealth of Nations*] Adam Smith's "invisible hand." The Prophet also has many sayings cherishing trade, profit making, and beauties of life. "Muhammad," as Maxime Rodinson put it simply, "was not a socialist."

Medieval Muslim Trade Routes

The conceptual openness of Islam towards business was one of the important reasons for the splendor of medieval Muslim civilization. The Islamic world was at the heart of global trade routes, and Muslim traders took advantage of this quite successfully. They even laid the foundations of some aspects of modern banking: instead of carrying heavy and easily stolen gold, medieval Muslim traders used paper checks. This innovation in credit transfer would be emulated and transferred to Europe by the Crusaders, particularly the Knights Templar.

So central was trade to Muslim civilization that its very decline may be attributed to changes in the pattern of global trade. When [Portuguese explorer] Vasco de Gama rounded the Cape of Good Hope in November 1497—thanks in part to the astrolabe, invented by Muslims—he opened a new chapter in world history, one in which global trade would shift from the Middle East and the Mediterranean to the oceans. Consequently the Arabic Middle East, which had been scorched by the Mongols two centuries before and could have never recovered anyway, entered deadly stagnation. The Ottoman Empire would excel for a few more centuries, but decline was inevitable. The loss of trade also meant the end of cosmopolitanism; this was followed by the rise of religious bigotry. While the early commentators of the Koran cherished trade and wealth as God's bounties, late Medieval Islamic literature began to emphasize extreme asceticism.

If things had not gone wrong, the business-friendly character of Islam could have well put it into the historical place of Calvinism, which, as [German political economist and sociologist] Max Weber persuasively argued, spearheaded the rise of capitalism. Weber himself wouldn't have agreed with this comment—he saw Islam as a religion of conquerors and plunderers, not hardworking laborers. According to Weber, Islam was an obstacle to capitalist development because it could foster only aggressive militancy (jihad) or contemplative austerity.

But Weber, in his *[Religion of China:] Confucianism and Taoism* (1915), argued that China could never breed a successful economy because its culture was too nepotistic. He was pretty pessimistic about Japan's potential for economic success, too. His analyses of these non-Christian civilizations failed because he assumed the perpetuity of their forms, and, in part, misread their histories. One of the greatest Turkish sociologists, Sabri F. Ülgener—both a student and a critic of Weber—wrote extensively about how he, despite his genius in analyzing the origins of capitalism in the West, misjudged Islam and overlooked its inherent compatibility with a "liberal market system."

The Historical Ban on Interest Taking

However this compatibility is not fully unproblematic. Among the aspects of modern capitalism, there is one particular bone of contention with Islam: interest. "Allah has permitted trade", the Koran commends, "and He has forbidden riba." And riba is generally translated as taking interest from money.

That's why modern Muslims have developed "Islamic banking" as an alternative to interest-based banking. This is, in fact, a transplantation of "venture capital" as it has been

An Early Muslim Economist Was Familiar with Supply and Demand

Occupying a unique place in intellectual history, Ibn Khaldun was a medieval historian, historiographer, sociologist and economist who lived in Tunis, Granada, and Egypt in the fourteenth century. Largely written out of Western intellectual history—Joseph Schumpeter [European economist and political scientist] slandered Islamic scholarship by arguing that there existed a 'great gap' between the Greek scholars and the Christian scholastics—Ibn Khaldun deserves a central place in economic thought.

Indeed, Imad A. Ahmad [president of Islamic public policy institute Minaret of Freedom] argues forcefully that Adam Smith was 'simply picking up where Ibn Khaldun left off'. Ibn Khaldun's writings display a clear and unambiguous familiarity with many of the central tenets of what we know as classical economic thought —for instance, an appreciation of supply and demand, of causality, and an understanding of the difference between normative and positive analysis.

His support for the labour theory of value—the theory that the value of something is determined by the amount of labour that has gone into its production—is an open academic question. However, Ahmad convincingly argues that he had a strong appreciation of subjective value—a good's value is solely determined by how much people are willing to pay for it—which would place him even higher on the intellectual hierarchy than many of the great nineteenth- and twentieth-century economists. . . .

Chris Berg and Andrew Kemp,
"Islam's Free Market Heritage,"
IPA Review *(Australia), March 2007.*

developed in the West; aspects of Islamic banking are adaptations of related services like leasing, partnership, mark-up financing and profit sharing.

While Islamic banking allows capitalism without interest, some Muslims go further and ask whether riba really includes reasonable interest. This liberal interpretation dates to the 16th century in the Ottoman Empire. During the reign of the Suleiman the Magnificent, his Sheik-ul Islam (Head of Islamic Affairs), Ebusuud Effendi, granted permission for the collection of interest by foundations working for the betterment of the society. In modern times, there are many Muslim scholars who have reinterpreted riba. Imad-ad-Dean Ahmad of the Minaret of Freedom Institute, for example, argues that the term actually means any unconscionable overcharging, whether on an interest rate or a spot price. Charging a market rate of interest, he holds, does not constitute riba.

Radical Islam Opposes Western Capitalism

Whether reasonable interest is allowed or not, Islam's theological and historical attitude towards business is undoubtedly positive. "The alleged fundamental opposition of Islam to capitalism," as Maxime Rodinson put it, "is a myth."

If this is so, whence comes "the battle between Islam and capitalism" as envisioned by radical Islamists like [Egyptian author and influential member of the Egyptian Muslim Brotherhood, Sayyid] Qutb?

The answer lies both in the asceticism of late Medieval Muslim thought, which remains alive today among many ultra-conservative Muslims, and in the un-Islamic origins of Islamic radicalism. The latter was born as an anti-colonialist, reactionary movement, and its main aim has been to create a socio-political system to challenge and defeat the West. Since the West was built on democratic capitalism, Islamic radicals argued that its opponents must adopt an alternative political/economic vision. That's why the founding fathers of radical

Islam—such as Qutb and [Pakistani journalist, theologian, and political philosopher, Sayyid Abul A'la] Mawdudi—borrowed heavily from what [writers and academics] Ian Buruma and Avi Margalit call "Occidentalism"—an ideology with its origins in [German philosopher Martin] Heidegger's criticism of the West, adopted by Japanese fascists, the Nazis, the Khmer Rouge and, more recently, Al Qaeda and their ilk.

The Desire for Prosperity in Turkey

Yet for those Muslims whose lives revolve not around Occidentalism but around personal religiosity and a natural human desire for the good life, democratic capitalism seems quite well suited.

Some striking examples of this phenomenon have emerged in Turkey in the past two decades. Turkey is not the richest country in the Islamic world, but it is arguably the most developed. The richest are the oil-rich Arab nations, most of which, despite their petro-dollars, remain socially pre-modern and tribal. Regrettably, oil brings wealth, but it does not modernize. Modernization comes through rationality, which can be achieved only through organization, order, exchange, and risk-taking in pursuit of goals. The late Turgut Özal, one of Turkey's wiser presidents, once said, "We are lucky that we don't have oil; we have to work hard to make money."

Özal was a pro-Western politician and a Muslim believer. His revolutionary, Reaganesque reforms during the 1980s transformed the Turkish economy from quasi-socialism to capitalism. In this new setting, the conservative Muslim masses of Anatolia [the part of modern Turkey that is in Asia] have found fertile ground for a socio-economic boom. Thanks to their astounding successes in business, they have been called "Anatolian Tigers." They constitute a new class that rivals the long-established, privileged, highly secularized and utterly condescending "Istanbul bourgeoisie."

The European Stability Initiative (ESI), a Berlin-based think tank, conducted an extensive study of the "Anatolian tigers" in 2005. ESI researchers interviewed hundreds of conservative businessmen in the central Anatolian city of Kayseri. They discovered that "individualistic, pro-business currents have become prominent within Turkish Islam," and a "quiet Islamic Reformation" was taking place in the hands of Muslim entrepreneurs. The term they used to define these godly capitalists was also the title of their report: "Islamic Calvinists."

The incumbent Justice and Development Party (AKP), seems to be a political echo of this rising "Islamic Calvinism" in Turkey. Most AKP members come from business backgrounds, and the party has been quite pro-business from its very first day. Its leader, [Turkey's] Prime Minister [Recep Tayyip] Erdogan, has repeatedly welcomed foreign direct investment from all countries—including Israel. Recently, in a speech given at an international Islamic conference, Mr. Erdogan called on Arab leaders to redefine the Islamic ban on interest and warned that Islamic banking could turn into a "trap" that might hinder development in the Muslim world. The more such voices are raised by Muslim leaders, scholars and intellectuals, the freer markets—and minds—will become in the broader Middle East.

Distinguishing Capitalism from Materialism

Still, many Muslims—in Turkey and elsewhere—despise capitalism and perceive it as something both alien and destructive to Islam. Yet this is a misdirected disdain. When you look at anti-capitalist rhetoric in Muslim circles, you will see that it is focused on sexual laxity, prostitution, drugs, crime, or the general selfishness in Western societies. Yet these are not the inherent elements of capitalism; they would be better explained by the term "cultural materialism"—the idea that material things are the only things that matter. Most Muslims who abhor capitalism simply confuse it with materialism.

Such worried Muslims would be quite surprised to discover that some of the most outspoken advocates of the free market in the West are also staunch defenders of religious faith, family values and the healthy role of both in public life. Unfortunately, the synthesis of democratic capitalism with Judeo-Christian values—which is basically an American, not a European phenomenon—is not well known in the Islamic world. The America of churches and charities is poorly represented in the global mass media. Quite the contrary, what most Muslims see as standard Americans are the unabashed hedonists of MTV and Hollywood.

In other words, not all capitalists are of the flock of Mammon [Christian, Biblical term defined as wealth or greed]. The more Muslims realize this, the less they will fear opening their societies to economic development, and the more they will remember the Koranic command, "Spread through the earth and seek God's bounty and remember God much so that hopefully you will be successful."

Then the world will be a much safer place, for a morally guided quest for capital is far more peaceful than a hate-driven "battle" against it.

| "Islamic extremism is a menace to the value of freedom."

Radical Islam Is Not Compatible with Modern Western Values

Magdi Khalil

In the following viewpoint, Magdi Khalil argues radical Islam is directly opposed to modern Western values, such as separation of church and state, freedom of expression, and sanctity of life. He cites examples of ways in which Muslims living in Western societies have continued to practice behaviors and rituals that are illegal under the laws of these societies. Further, he contends that radical Islam has sought to alter United Nations human rights guidelines to suit its own view of the world, thereby attempting to limit freedom of speech in other countries. Khalil is the executive editor of the Watani International, *an Egyptian weekly publication, and a columnist for the London-based daily newspaper* Asharq Al-Awsat.

Magdi Khalil, "Modernity and Western Values in the Clutches of Islamization," *Contemporary Review*, vol. 288, Autumn 2006, pp. 345–349. Copyright © 2006 Contemporary Review Company Ltd. Reproduced by the permission of Contemporary Review Company Ltd.

As you read, consider the following questions:

1. According to the author, to what aspects of life and society have Muslim militants attached the label "Islamic" and for what purpose?

2. What are some of the Western values that the author identifies as being incompatible with Islam?

3. What does the author believe to be the potential consequences if the United Nations Commission on Human Rights adds to its guidelines the clause suggested by the Muslim states?

The Danish cartoons [negatively depicting the prophet Mohammed and Islam in September 2005] that greatly offended the Muslim world ... have probably sparked an even greater debate about how the Muslims interact with the contemporary world. Muslim reformers of the past century—such as Mohammed Abdu, Refaa Al-Tahtawi, Taha Hussein, Ali Abdel-Razik and others—sought and unfortunately failed to modernize Islam.

The militants, led by Hassan Al-Banna and his partisans, won this battle, and forced their vision to 'Islamize' modernity on the people. They created a certain pattern—a mindset and a lifestyle—and promoted it as 'The Valid Islam,' *Al Islam al-Sahih*. They resorted to seduction and fear to impose this pattern on their societies and made sure to attach an 'Islamic' label to each and every aspect, with the clear implication that other patterns were deemed non-Muslim and illegitimate.

An increasingly wide array of things fall under this valid pattern: the Islamic dress, the Islamic banks, the Islamic economy, the Islamic education, the Islamization of science, the media and the judiciary system, the application and enforcement of Islamic laws, the widespread dissemination of the fundamentalist culture, the promotion of Islamic medicine and the Prophet's medicine, the expansion of Islamic organizations, the marginalization of the national identity of the state in favour of Islamic nationalism, and the Islamization of daily vocabulary and political terms (*mobayaa* [pledge of allegiance], *welaya* [governance], *shura* [counsel], *thawabet al-oma* [contestants], etc.).

Muslim Immigrants to the West Reject Modernity

As a result, the Muslim countries wasted their chance to embrace modernity, opting instead to import a shallow veneer of modernity from the West; and they became idle consumers of the products of civilization, with no contributions to offer. With different factions engaging in a morbid religious bid, intent on proving that they can win the title of the most rigid fundamentalists, it is no wonder that the Muslim societies started to crumble from within under the mounting pressures of regression and strife. However, the damage did not stop there, as some of those bidders developed a terrifying propensity towards violence which left a hideous mark on their societies; then, in a moment that went down in history, the violence spilled out to the outside world, and thus began the Muslims' greatest crisis with the contemporary world, and particularly with the West.

If this horrifying action brought about the initial problem, the crisis became more pronounced as a result of the massive Muslim immigration to Western countries, and the presence of large Muslim communities in Europe, the United States and Australia. These communities are supposed to bridge the modernity gap between West and East as the pioneers of the Arab renaissance once did, but, instead, many of the immigrants are holding firm to the prospect of Islamized modernity, whether because of a long-ingrained belief or one acquired through the influence of the Islamized media stemming, in over-abundance, from the Middle East. Many have insulated themselves in their own world, in a form of isolated 'ghettos', identified by their particular dress, *halal* food [permitted for consumption under Islamic law] and special culture.

Disobeying Western Laws in Favor of Religious Ideals

In and of itself, this poses no problem, as the modern Western mind-set greatly values pluralism and respects cultural idiosyncrasies. However, it soon became a problem when some of those immigrants attempted to impose their own values on the Western societies in which they lived, or to elevate their values above the laws of the communities in which they lived. United States Vice President Dick Cheney summed up the situation by saying: 'Either the Islamist terrorists will succeed to alter the Western lifestyle, or the West will succeed in altering their lifestyle'.

On the Islamic side, the European Muslim advocate Tariq Ramadan, who has recently lectured in Britain, confirmed without hesitation: 'The Muslims should not accept values that conflict with the Islamic faith and values', and 'The Muslims are not obliged to uphold the secular French tradition; they have made no historical contributions to this tradition'.

But what happens when those values clash with the law? What about spreading hatred in the name of religion, beating women (as the *Imam* of a mosque in Spain encouraged), female circumcision, the violation of children's rights, polygamy, judging non-Muslims as infidels, deeming the Muslims' enlistment in Western militaries an illegitimate act, abusing the system of social welfare, heaping praise on terrorism and acts of murder, or actually joining terrorist organizations?

Islam Does Not Recognize the Separation Between Church and State

A major difference in opinion between the Muslims and the West has to do with the separation of state and religion, in-

Religious Enclaves May Supersede the U.S. Constitution

First in Europe and now in the United States, Muslim groups have petitioned to establish enclaves in which they can uphold and enforce greater compliance to Islamic law. While the U.S. Constitution enshrines the right to religious freedom and the prohibition against a state religion, when it comes to the rights of religious enclaves to impose communal rules, the dividing line is more nebulous. Can U.S. enclaves, homeowner associations, and other groups enforce Islamic law?

Such questions are no longer theoretical. While Muslim organizations first established enclaves in Europe, the trend is now crossing the Atlantic. Some Islamist community leaders in the United States are challenging the principles of assimilation and equality once central to the civil rights movement, seeking instead to live according to a separate but equal philosophy. The Gwynnoaks Muslim Residential Development group, for example, has established an informal enclave in Baltimore, Maryland. . . .

David Kennedy Houck,
"The Islamist Challenge to the U.S. Constitution,"
Middle East Quarterly, *Spring 2006.*

cluding the right to criticize religions, and the right to have a religious belief, or to hold no religious beliefs (atheism). It was this total and clear-cut separation of religion and state that made the members of the European Union insist on not making a single reference to Christianity in the European constitution, though it is the recognized faith of the majority in Europe.

There are countless books in Europe that attack religion, God, the prophets and Christianity in particular, and many that proclaim atheism. Karl Marx [a founder of communism], the man whose philosophy depended on the statement that 'religion was the opium of the people' embraced atheism as a foundation for his ideology. The famous German philosopher Nietzsche went as far as saying that 'God is dead'; the French existentialist [Jean-Paul] Sartre and his rebellious, atheist philosophy comes to mind, as well as dozens of variable atheist schools and philosophies that have spread throughout Europe. People are unlikely to forget shocking novels and movies such as *The Last Temptation of Christ, The Da Vinci Code, The Abnormality of Paul* [the latter of] which discredited St. Paul, and even more shocking the book entitled *The Foolishness of God.* Yet, there are no reports about anyone losing his life as a penalty for criticizing Christianity, and these philosophies and books did not jeopardize Christianity or Judaism; as a matter of fact, the Eastern bloc countries went right back to their abandoned faith after the collapse of the USSR.

Killing in the Name of Religion

Islamic extremism is a menace to the value of freedom, starting with the murderous threats against the novelist Salman Rushdie, the murders of the Egyptian intellectual Farag Fouda and the Dutch filmmaker Theo van Gogh; and ending recently with the *fatwa* (legal Islamic opinion) to kill the Danish cartoonist and the riots and acts of violence that surrounded this incident. In between the first and the latest, there were dozens of incidents when writers, intellectuals and artists were the target of similar assaults. Following the publication of the cartoons, a *fatwa* [legal pronouncement] sanctioned the elimination of the cartoonist, and a statement by *al-Aksa* Martyrs Brigades in Palestine threatened the citizens of Denmark, Norway and France. *Sheikh* Hassan Nasrallah, the head of the extremist *Hezbollah* movement, said that people would not have dared to insult the Prophet if the novelist Salman Rushdie had been executed. Nasrallah is now much better known after his recent war with Israel.

Nasrallah's appalling comment echoes that of Omar Abdel Rahman [Egyptian Muslim leader known as the Blind Sheikh] years ago: "If Naguib Mahfouz 'the Egyptian author Nobel-laureate' had been killed, Salman Rushdie wouldn't have crossed the line". Abdel Rahman has thus given his blessings for killing Naguib Mahfouz, who received a serious injury in a failed attempt on his life. The frenzy surrounding this last incident was palpable when an Islamic demonstration went out in London carrying terrorist slogans that incite hatred and murder and defied the basic values of Western civilization: 'To hell with freedom', 'Slay those who insult the prophet', 'Wipe out those who mock Islam', 'Europe, you will pay the price: The disaster of 9/11 is on its way to you'.

The Islamic Double Standard

Meanwhile, the Arab media has no qualms about attacking and insulting Christianity and Judaism. Let's take a look at some insulting titles written by Abu Islam Ahmed, the Egyptian Islamic writer, that were displayed in The Cairo International Book Fair in January 2006: *The Church and Sexual Deviation, Pagan Beliefs in Christianity, The Unholy Book, A Nation Without a Cross, Oh ye filthy gypsies: a message to the Diaspora Christians*; and a book about Farag Fouda, under the extremely revolting title *Who Killed the Dog?*

The most prominent Arab newspaper *Al-Ahram* devotes a whole page every week to the articles of Zaghloul Al-Nagar, where, among other things, he openly expresses the contempt he has for other religions: 'Judaism is not so much a religion as it is a disease that twists the sane human nature and takes it out of the circle of humanity and into the devils' circle' (*Al-Ahram*, 22 July 2002), 'the infidels and hypocrite unbelievers are mainly those among *Ahl-Al-ketab* (People of the Book, i.e.

Jews and Christians) who have corrupted their religion, the vile Jews, the worst infidels throughout history and until God inherits the land' (*Al-Ahram*, 15 July, 2002).

The insults are not just restricted to the written word, but extend to extremely rude actions as reported by a *Los Angeles Times* journalist who saw a number of Palestinians who were hiding in the 'Nativity' church use pages from the Holy Bible as toilet paper. However, no Muslims were assaulted due to this incident, and there were no violent demonstrations in the West, a fact that stands in sharp contrast with the Muslims' increasingly frenzied reaction, the excessive threats and the actual violence whenever Islam is involved.

An Attempt To Force the World To Submit to Islamist Fascism

The Muslim states have collectively requested the following statement be included in the proposal to establish a human rights council as a substitute for the UN [United Nations] Human Rights Commission: 'An offence directed at religions or prophets should be considered a threat to human rights and basic freedoms, and is in conflict with the freedom of expression'. If the statement is approved, freedom will be imperiled, mouths will be gagged, and the militants and extremists will be celebrating their victory, while the world will be forced to bow to the values of Islamist Fascism.

First, the Muslim countries will not abide by this resolution, just as they did not abide by other UN resolutions and treaties; second, they do not acknowledge other religions (for example Denmark acknowledges twelve religions, while most Muslim states only acknowledge three religions, and some of them only acknowledge Islam, and realistically, in all of the Muslim countries, the Muslims are the only ones to enjoy religious freedom as defined by the UN); third, followers of religions other than Islam suffer the most persecution in the Muslim states; fourth, while the Muslim states are halfheartedly condemning terrorism, they are in fact backing terrorists and supporting their tactics. At the end of the road, terrorism will benefit the most from this 'protection'; this clause will shield it against criticism since Islamic terrorism resorts to religious texts as a means to mobilize and motivate terrorists.

The call for an international law that restricts individual freedoms is an open invitation for fascism to set roots and take over the world; fascist values were behind the regression of the Muslim societies, and it is illogical to impose those same values on countries which have bravely resisted fascism, Nazism, and religious tyranny, and paid the price with the lives of millions of victims.

The shameful silence of the moderate Muslims in Muslim states will eventually make the leadership of those states fall into the hands of the militants, corrupted opportunists, and tyrants; it will also increase the chances of a disastrous collision with the path of progress of humanity. Ultimately, the values of freedom will gain the upper hand, but it seems that humanity is once more about to pay a huge price in order to preserve those values, and this time the face-off is with militant Islam.

Periodical Bibliography

The following articles have been selected to supplement the diverse views presented in this chapter.

Geneive Abdo — "False Prophets," *Foreign Policy*, July-August 2008.

Shahram Akbarzadeh — "Reinterpreting Islam," *Eureka Street*, April 11, 2008.

Maha Azzam — "In the Name of Islam," *World Today*, August 2008.

Rogier van Bakel — "The Trouble Is the West," *Reason*, November 2007.

Joseph Farah — "Are We at War with Islam?" WorldNetDaily, June 25, 2002. www.wnd.com.

Brian Handwerk — "Can Islam and Democracy Coexist?" National Geographic News, October 24, 2003. http://news.nationalgeographic.com.

Tom Holland — "Europe's First Revolution," *New Statesman*, October 13, 2008.

Terence P. Jeffrey — "Clash of Civilizations Is Also a Clash of Faith," *Human Events*, June 18, 2007.

Zvika Krieger — "Mecca Bucks," *New Republic*, March 26, 2008.

Damien Pieretti — "Islamism and Democracy in Egypt: Converging Paths?" *Washington Report on Middle East Affairs*, March 2008.

Tirza Visser — "When Islam and Democracy Meet: Muslims in Europe and the United States," *International Journal of Public Theology*, 2008.

OPPOSING
VIEWPOINTS®
SERIES

CHAPTER 2

Does Islam Promote Violence?

Chapter Preface

Many years after the advent of Islam in the seventh century, Muslim *fuqaha*, interpreters and experts in Islamic law, coined the terms *dar al-Islam* (house of Islam) and *dar al-Harb* (house of war). *Dar al-Islam* refers to countries where Muslims can practice Islam safely and peacefully and those that share a common border with another Muslim country. However, a country cannot be considered part of *dar al-Islam* simply because the majority of its population is Muslim. The distinction *dar al-Islam* is actually one of a legal rather than theological nature. A country must be ruled by *sharia*, or Islamic law, for it to be considered part of the house of Islam, and the rights of Muslims are assumed to be secure throughout the *dar al-Islam*.

Regions considered *dar al-harb* are those that do not follow *sharia* law and are therefore failing to follow the will of Allah. As a result, those not submitting to Allah are thought to be in a state of war and rebellion, and Muslims living in these regions are thought to be living insecure lives. Followers of Islam are expected to spread Allah's message, by force if necessary, and many believe any resistance by regions that are considered *dar al-harb* should be met with jihad, holy struggle, because *dar al-harb* is the source of all strife in the world.

Several Western critics use the distinction of *dar-al harb* and the corresponding Muslim duty to jihad against it to suggest that Islam is a violent religion. In an article for *Middle East Quarterly*, David Bukay, a lecturer at the University of Haifa, Israel, states, "Jihad both purifies the *dar al-Islam* and is the tool to shrink and eradicate the *dar al-harb*. As a doctrine, the aim of jihad is clear: to establish God's rule on earth by compelling non-Muslims to embrace Islam, or to force them to accept second-class status if not eradicate them altogether." These critics often point out modern Muslim authorities who support a militant notion of jihad by referring to the partition between the house of Islam and the house of war.

Other Muslim scholars, however, view the division as outdated and inapplicable to the modern world. Imam Abduljalid Sajid, the chairman of the Muslim Council for Religious and Racial Harmony in the United Kingdom, notes that "It is evident today that in many 'Muslim' countries Muslims' lives, honour and right to follow Islam are not safe while there are 'non-Muslim' countries, like our own country, where Muslims' lives and properties are safe legally. Moreover, we enjoy legal rights to follow our religion and preach it. Therefore, it is a mistake to apply the old concept of *dar al-Islam* and *dar al-Harb* on the contemporary world."

Because *dar al-Islam* and *dar al-harb* are concepts derived from Islamic law and not from the Qur'an, their relevance to modern understandings of Islam is still in question. As the viewpoints in the following chapter emphasize, many of the claims of Islam's peaceful or violent nature similarly depend on how one interprets Islamic scripture and its applicability to a rapidly globalizing world.

| *"The mortal threat we face is jihadism, which is caused by Islam."*

The Islamic Doctrine of Jihad Advocates Violence

Andrew C. McCarthy

In the viewpoint that follows, Andrew C. McCarthy states the ji-had—or holy struggle—advocated by radical Islam is by defini-tion violent. Additionally, he states this violence has roots in Is-lamic doctrine and history. McCarthy believes the United States must accept that jihad is not a personal striving—as some Mus-lim apologists claim—but a doctrine to incite individuals to harm the United States and its allies. McCarthy serves as the di-rector of the Center for Law and Counterterrorism at the Foun-dation for Defense of Democracies and is author of the book Willful Blindness: A Memoir of the Jihad.

As you read, consider the following questions:

1. According to the author, what are the current and his-toric Islamic definitions of jihad?

2. How many people does McCarthy estimate the ideals of jihad represent within the Muslim population?

Andrew C. McCarthy, "The Jihad in Plain Sight," Hudson Institute, May 6, 2008. Repro-duced by permission. www.hudson.org.

3. Does the author believe the United States has taken the jihadist enemy seriously in the past, and has this attitude changed since the terrorist attacks of September 11, 2001?

The left is in full swoon over . . . restaurant menus.

For well-meaning progressives, there is, of course, no war on terror. The "war"—at least this week's "war"—is on obesity. Thus, with barely contained glee, the *New York Times* reported on April 17 [2008] that a federal judge had upheld the regulation, promulgated by the Health Commissioner of [New York City] Mayor Michael Bloomberg's Nanny City, requiring all eateries to post a calorie-count for each menu offering.

Disgruntled restaurateurs had groused that they knew best how to serve their patrons, and that the patrons were adult enough to make their own choices. The Commissioner, though, would have none of it. He urged the court that this battle of the bulge was a crisis. In such straits, he declaimed, nothing is more crucial than information. Judge Richard J. Holwell agreed. Edified about their interests, it seemed to the jurist only natural that "consumers will use the information to select lower-calorie meals," and that "these choices will lead to a lower incidence of obesity."

Alas, information turns out to be crucial only in a manufactured crisis. When it comes to the real thing, like the jihadist threat to our lives and our way of life, we'd prefer not to know.

Removal of "Jihad" from the Public Lexicon

That is the clear message from our diplomatic progressives at Foggy Bottom [the Washington, D.C., neighborhood where the U.S. Department of State headquarters is located]. A week after Judge Holwell issued his calorie-count decision from the very courthouse that served throughout the nineties as front-line in what then passed for the war against jihadism, the

[George W.] Bush administration circulated guidance, long touted by the State Department and other pockets of Islamophilia, that would purge *jihadism*—the word, the very thought—from our public lexicon.

The Surgeon General believes smokers need a neon warning of the pluperfectly obvious. State, however, does not think jihadism is hazardous to your health. To the contrary, our top policy makers—the officials who regard [chairman of the Palestine Liberation Organization and president of the Palestinian National Authority until his death on November 11, 2004] Yasser Arafat's legacy, Fatah [The Palestinian National Liberation movement, dedicated to securing a national state of Palestine] as an indispensable partner for peace; who've just responded [in 2008] to the news that North Korea is helping Syria build nukes by . . . removing [leader of North Korea] Kim Jong-il's terror regime from the perennial list of State Sponsors of Terrorism—have determined that jihad, like Islam itself, is a public good and therefore (try to follow this) we should just stop talking about it.

We Western non-Muslims, you see, must school the world's 1.4 billion adherents of Islam: The "real" jihad is an internal struggle for personal betterment, a key tenet of the Religion of Peace—or the "religion of love and peace," the iteration preferred by Secretary of State Condoleezza Rice at the annual Iftaar dinner by which official Washington now marks the end of the "holy month of Ramadan." Besides, administration officials helpfully explained to the Associated Press, referring to a terrorist as a *jihadist*, an *Islamo-fascist*, or a *mujahideen* "may actually boost support for radicals among Arab and Muslim audiences by giving them a veneer of religious credibility or by causing offense to moderates."

A Concept of Western Intellectuals

Of course, if *jihad* truly were a sublime summons to become a better person, it is not entirely clear how plowing jumbo jets into skyscrapers and mass-murdering civilians could achieve the sheen of the sacerdotal [of priests] in the eyes of the faith-ful—droves of whom took to the streets in celebration of the 9/11 atrocities. Nor is it clear why calling a terrorist a jihadist would cause angst for "moderates" . . . unless they are pre-tending that *jihad* is something other than what it is.

And they are. In so doing, moreover, they enjoy enormous support from special pleaders strategically dotted throughout government, to say nothing of their academy and media allies. Yet, as I've recently documented in *Willful Blindness: A Mem-oir of the Jihad*, for all its energetic earnestness, the campaign to refurbish *jihad* (and to crush dissenters) is persuasive only in the ivory towers of elites desperate to be persuaded. Down here on Planet Earth, it is futile.

The Muslim world is not populated by Western intellectu-als hard-wired to nuance white into black by legalistic arcana and historical massaging. In large swaths of the ummah [Arab world], there is rampant illiteracy, education consists of myo-pic focus on the Qur'an, and intolerance (especially anti-Semitism) is so rudimentary a part of everyday life that any jihad rooted in "good works in society" would not conceivably comport with Western liberals' understanding of that term.

Progressive, moderate Muslims would doubtless like the concept of jihad to vanish. They are in a battle for authentic-ity with fundamentalists, and jihad would be far easier to omit than it is to explain away. Indeed, if anyone should re-sort to a purge of *jihad*, better it be Muslim reformers repeal-ing the concept than U.S. Pollyannas striking the word. To persist in conceding jihad's centrality as an Islamic obligation while distorting its essence can only fatally damage the reformers' credibility and, hence, the entire reform effort.

Jihad Is Deeply Rooted in Islam

Jihad, however, is very unlikely to go away. There are too many Muslims who believe in it, and there would be no Mus-lim world without it. When it comes to jihad, authenticity is simplicity, and, simply stated, jihad is and has always been about forcible conquest. As explicated by the West's pre-eminent scholar of Islam, Princeton's Bernard Lewis:

> Conventionally translated "holy war" [*jihad*] has the literal meaning of striving, more specifically, in the Qur'anic phrase "striving in the path of God" (*fi sabil Allah*). Some Muslim theologians, particularly in more modern times, have interpreted the duty of "striving in the path of God" in a spiritual and moral sense. The overwhelming majority of early authorities, however, citing relevant passages in the Qur'an and in the tradition, discuss jihad in military terms.

In fact, the erudite former Muslim of the *nom de plume* [pen name] Ibn Warraq points out that even

> [t]he celebrated *Dictionary of Islam* defines *jihad* as a religious war with those who are unbelievers in the mission of Muhammad. It is an incumbent religious duty, established in the Quran and in the Traditions as a divine institution, enjoined specially for the purpose of advancing Islam and of repelling evil from Muslims.

It is no wonder that this should be so. The Qur'an repeatedly enjoins Muslims to fight and slay non-Muslims. "O ye who believe," commands Sura 9:123, "fight those of the disbelievers who are near you, and let them find harshness in you, and know that Allah is with those who keep their duty unto him." It is difficult to spin that as a call to spiritual self-improvement. As it is, to take another example, with Sura 9:5: "But when the forbidden months are past, then fight and slay the pagans wherever ye find them. And seize them, beleaguer them, and lie in wait for them in every stratagem (of war)," relenting only if they have accepted Islam. The *hadith*, lengthy volumes recording the words and traditions of the prophet, are even more explicit, as in Mohammed's teaching that "[a] single endeavor (of fighting) in Allah's cause in the afternoon or in the forenoon is better than all the world and whatever is in it."

A U.S.-Produced Cold War Textbook Advocated Violent Jihad

In the twilight of the Cold War, the United States spent millions of dollars to supply Afghan schoolchildren with textbooks filled with violent images and militant Islamic teachings, part of covert attempts to spur resistance to the Soviet occupation.

The primers, which were filled with talk of *jihad* and featured drawings of guns, bullets, soldiers and mines, have served since then as the Afghan school system's core curriculum. Even the Taliban used the American-produced books. . . .

What seemed like a good idea in the context of the Cold War is being criticized by humanitarian workers as a crude tool that steeped a generation in violence.

Joe Stephens and David B. Ottaway,
"From U.S., the ABC's of Jihad: Violent Soviet-Era
Textbooks Complicate Afghan Education Efforts,"
Washington Post, *March 23, 2002.*

A Candid Discussion of Jihad and Islam Is Necessary

It is an unrelenting fact that Islamic doctrine is the catalyst for the cataracts of Islamic terror raining down on the globe. This does not mean all or most Muslims are or will become terrorists—though some percentage will, and a far larger number will sympathize with fundamentalist goals if not terrorist methods. Nor does it mean that Islamic doctrine is not rife with many virtuous, peaceable elements—though many of these, their resonance with Western intellectuals notwithstanding, trace to the initial, Meccan phase of the Mohammed's ministry, borrowing heavily from other religious traditions as the prophet sought to entice conversion to the new creed; they were later superseded by the bellicose scriptures of the Medinan period, when the warrior prophet spread Islam by the sword.

What it does mean, though, is that the mortal threat we face *is* jihadism, which *is caused by Islam*—no less than obesity is caused by high calorie counts, lung cancer by smoking cigarettes, birth defects by imbibing alcohol during pregnancy, and countless lesser risks to our well-being by pathologies our benevolent bureaucrats compel us to confront remorselessly (unconcerned that they might be misconstrued as crusading to rid the world of food, tobacco, alcohol, etc.).

No less do we require accurate information about jihadism to arrive at sound public policy.

Because discussions of this topic are so infected by timidity, passion and no small amount of demagoguery, it bears emphasis that there is no single Islam. In marked contrast to most Judeo-Christian traditions regnant in the West, Islam is bereft of a regimented clerical hierarchy, councils, or synods to provide standards of orthodoxy. Though the Sunni/Shiite divide draws most of our attention, there is in fact a wide variety of Islamic sects, to say nothing of the prevalent phenomenon—quite familiar to Westerners—of adherents who are at best culturally or nominally Muslim but care little about theology and its demands. That said, however, it is whistling past the graveyard to ignore or minimize the virulent strain of fundamentalist Islam that galvanizes jihadism. And it is positively fatuous to suggest that it stems from what Americans say about it. Witness, to take just one recent example, the rioting jihadists in Indonesia who stoned and burned a . . . mosque—their anger provoked by another sect of Muslims, the Ahmadi, who are deemed heretics because they don't accept Mohammed as the final prophet or jihad as a divine injunction.

It is simply not the case that a mere nineteen terrorists hijacked a peaceful religion, as President [George W.] Bush hastened to assure Americans while smoke billowed from the Pentagon and lifeless bodies were pulled from the rubble of the Twin Towers. It is not the case, as the Clinton administration and its Justice Department were equally emphatic in mollifying the public when the World Trade Center [WTC] was first bombed in 1993, that a rag-tag handful of miscreants had "perverted" the "true Islam." The species of Islam that has spurred these and other attacks has a long and distinguished pedigree. It is fourteen centuries old. It is rooted in the literal commands of the scriptures. It is a project that has engaged high intellects, and a belief system that continues to win the allegiance of the educated and the illiterate, rich and poor, young and old, princes and peons—cutting even across the Sunni/Shiite divide. It is not the majority construction of the faith, but it is the creed of a sizable minority—and a dynamic one, underwritten by Saudi [Arabian] billions and catapulted by [Iranian revolutionary and then Ayatollah Ruhollah Musavi] Khomeini's revolution. Even if it were representative of only twenty percent of the Muslim world (an estimate which probably sells it short), that would translate into over a quarter-billion people.

Propagation of Violent Jihad

For the past thirty years, Omar Abdel Rahman, the infamous "Blind Sheikh," has been among the most consequential exponents of this doctrinal interpretation. It is he who spurred the murderers of Egyptian President Anwar Sadat in 1981, the WTC bombers in 1993, and, according to al Qaeda leader Osama bin Laden, the 9/11 suicide hijackers. He is no perverter of scripture. To the contrary, he is better understood as a party-spoiling resister of modernization and anti-literalism. A doctor of Islamic jurisprudence graduated from al-Azhar

University in Egypt, the seat of Sunni learning, his renown as a master of doctrine accounts for his influence.

Jihad, he instructed hordes of admirers, is "the peak of a full [embrace] of Islam. . . . There is no work that equals" it. He recounted that, for over a millennium, jihad had unambiguously and unapologetically called for the aggressive application of brute force against oppressors and infidels. It "means fighting the enemies." Jihad was not about internal betterment, other efforts at peaceful achievement. It was not to be accomplished by such quotidian practices as prayer, mosque attendance, alms giving, or living a virtuous life. At such suggestions, he scoffed:

> Jihad is jihad. . . . There is no such thing as commerce, industry and science in jihad. This is calling things . . . other than by [their] own name. If God . . . says, "Do jihad," it means do jihad with the sword, with the cannon, with the grenades and with the missile. This is jihad. Jihad against God's enemies for God's cause and his word.

Echoing his most profound influences—fourteenth-century scholar Ibn Taymiyyah, the [Egyptian] Muslim Brotherhood's intellectual engine Sayyid Qutb, and Ayatollah Khomeini (a Shiite whose triumph in Iran Abdel Rahman hoped to replicate in Egypt and beyond)—the Blind Sheikh exhorted followers that it was their duty to wage jihad against any regime that did not govern by Allah's law, sharia. In the short term, this meant in Islamic countries; in the long term, because Islam aspires to global hegemony, it meant throughout the world.

The command is straight out of Qutb, who rejected as an absurdity that Islam's core mission could ever be achieved by individual efforts at personal betterment or the religion's intellectual force. Supplanting man's dominion with God's could never "be achieved only through preaching," he warned, because incumbent regimes were plainly "not going to give up their power merely through preaching." Expelling them was the mission of jihad, highlighting its centrality as a core Islamic obligation. The purpose of jihad is "to wipe out tyranny and to introduce freedom to mankind." Whenever Islam is obstructed by "the political system of the state, the socio-economic system based on races and classes, and behind all these, the military power of the government," the religion, according to Qutb, "has no recourse but to remove them by force so that when [Islam] is addressed to peoples' hearts and minds they are free to accept or reject it with an open mind." All such impediments are deemed to be persecution, implicating the Qur'anic injunction (in Sura 2:190–91) to "Fight in the cause of Allah those who fight you . . . and slay them whenever you catch them, and turn them out from where they have turned you out, for persecution is worse than slaughter."

There were blazing signs that Abdel Rahman's acolytes were preparing just such an offensive in the years before radical Islam declared war by bombing the World Trade Center in 1993. We refused to see them. The FBI ended surveillance in 1989 despite witnessing the nascent jihad army conducting paramilitary training. The CIA allowed its lavish aid for the Afghan mujahideen to flow to the most anti-American elements of the anti-Soviet jihad—elements that promptly turned on the United States once the Russians were defeated. A brazen 1990 killing by Abdel Rahman henchman Sayyid Nosair, the murder of Jewish Defense League founder Meir Kahane, was treated as the work of a lone, crazed gunman despite a wealth of seized evidence proving Nosair was part of a jihadist network which had far greater ambitions.

Getting Serious About Jihad

Simply stated, we did not take the enemy and his motivations seriously before he announced himself. We did not react seriously in attempting before 9/11 to prosecute him into submission while he attacked again and again. And we are not serious now if we believe we can democratize him into submission—a fact that should be palpable given his penchant for exploiting democratic freedoms in furthering the jihad, and given that lack of democracy is not what drives him to act. His motivation is what he takes to be the divine summons to jihad.

The jihadist project—and it most certainly is a *jihadist* project—is to remove all barriers to the establishment of sharia [Islamic law] (the prerequisite for Islam's dominance). Those barriers are not merely military but political, cultural, spiritual and attitudinal. Force is used when necessary, but the theory of terrorism—and, while barbarous, terrorism is a rational method, not a form of madness—is that force should rarely be necessary. The terrorist defies our settled assumptions about civilized behavior. His actions, quite intentionally, are wanton and depraved, the better to extort us into capitulation through occasional shock and awe rather than a regular, predictable pattern of attacks. Though his self-perception is hallow, the terrorist's strategy is not in principle different from the mafia loanshark, who generally collects his usurious payments without incident because the debtor well knows the wages of resistance.

> *"Jihad, properly understood, is a continuous action or process that animates every day and night of the life of the true believer."*

The Islamic Doctrine of Jihad Does Not Advocate Violence

Maulana Wahiduddin Khan

Jihad is a peaceful concept in Islam, which encourages the believer to continually strive for self-improvement, according to Maulana Wahiduddin Khan in the viewpoint that follows. Khan contends jihad is related to the peaceful path that Muhammed preferred to take whenever possible while he was alive. Additionally, the author states Islam as a religion recognizes the value of engaging in peaceful instead of violent acts and encourages its followers to follow this path. Khan is widely recognized as the spiritual ambassador of Islam to the world who advocates peace and interfaith cooperation and dialogue. He has written numerous books and is the recipient of many humanitarian awards.

As you read, consider the following questions:

1. According to Kahn, what does the concept of jihad encourage a Muslim to do when they encounter a nonbeliever?

Maulana Wahiduddin Khan, "The Concept of Jihad in Islam," *The American Muslim*, September 22, 2008. Reproduced by permission. http://theamericanmuslim.org.

2. What type of jihad does Khan state involves physical warfare?

3. What does the author identify as the three aspects of jihad?

The word 'jihad' is derived from the root juhd, which means 'to strive' or 'to struggle.' It denotes the exertion of oneself to the utmost, to the limits of one's capacity, in some activity or for some purpose. This is how the word is understood in Arabic grammar.

Because fighting against one's enemies is also one form of this exertion or striving, it is also sometimes referred to as jihad. However, the actual Arabic word for this is qital, not jihad. Fighting with one's enemies is something that might happen only occasionally or exceptionally. However, jihad, properly understood, is a continuous action or process that animates every day and night of the life of the true believer. Such a person does not let any hurdle affect his life, including desire for gain, the pressure of customs, the demands of pragmatism, lust for wealth, etc. All these things serve as hurdles in the path of doing good deeds. Overcoming these hurdles and yet abiding by the commandments of God is the true jihad, and this is the essential meaning of the concept of jihad. There are many references to jihad, as understood in this way, in the collections of sayings attributed to the Prophet Muhammad.

An Ideological Jihad

The present world is a testing ground, and its environment has been fashioned in such a way that human beings are constantly put to the test. In the course of this test, human beings are faced with numerous hurdles, to face which one must repeatedly suppress or sacrifice one's own desires or, in some cases, even one's own self. Overcoming these odds and facing all sorts of difficulties and losses but still remaining firm on the path of truth is the real and fundamental jihad. Those who remain steadfast in the path of this jihad will be blessed with entrance to paradise.

Jihad, in essence, is a form of peaceful action or activism. This peaceful activism can take the form of inviting others to the path of truth. The Quran advises us not to obey those who champion falsehood, and tells us to engage in jihad with them through the Quran. This means that one should respond to them by inviting them to the path of the truth, striving till one's utmost in this regard. The jihad that this Quranic verse refers to is not physical warfare. Rather, reference here is to intellectual and ideological activism. In short, it means refuting falsehood and advancing the cause of the truth [using peaceful means].

Qital, which is one form of jihad, involves physical warfare, but this also cannot be divorced from the issue of essentially peaceful jihad. If an enemy challenges one militarily or through physical force, one should still strive to the utmost possible to respond through peaceful means. Such means can be abandoned only when it is no longer possible to use them or when warfare becomes the only way to respond to the violence being unleashed.

In this regard a statement attributed to Hazrat Ayesha [one of the wives of the Prophet] serves as a guiding principle. This statement is contained in the *Sahih Bukhari*, a book of traditions attributed to the Prophet. She said that whenever the Prophet was faced with two choices, he would always opt for the easier one. This means that he would prefer the easier option and would ignore the harder option. This principle of the Prophet applied not only to routine affairs of life but also to serious matters such as war, which is itself a difficult option. A reading of the life of the Prophet reveals that he never initiated fighting on his own. Whenever his foes sought to force him into battle, he would always try to seek some means to avoid physical fighting. He engaged in fighting only when all other options were closed. Thus, as the Prophet's practice reveals, offensive war is forbidden in Islam. Islam allows only for defensive war, and that too only when this becomes absolutely unavoidable.

Muhammed Chose Peace Whenever Possible

In reality, in life one is always faced with the dilemma of making choices between different options. Some options are based on peace, others on violence. The accounts of the Prophet's life indicate that in every matter he preferred the former. A few instances from his life are in order to illustrate this fact:

Soon after being appointed as a prophet, he was faced with a choice between the two sorts of options. His mission was to end polytheism and to establish pure monotheism, belief in and surrender to the one God. The Kaaba [the most sacred site in Islam] in Mecca had originally been made as a centre for the worship of the one God, but by the time of the advent of the Prophet some 360 idols had been installed therein. Hence, one might think that in the Quran the Prophet should have first been instructed to purify the Kaaba of the idols and to remake it as a centre for monotheism. But had this been the case, this would have been tantamount to warring with the Qureish of Mecca, who enjoyed leadership among the Arabs [as their most dominant tribe] precisely because they were custodians of the Kaaba. History tells us that [at this stage] the Prophet restricted himself simply to spreading the message of monotheism instead of removing the idols from the Kaaba. This, in a sense, is a major instance of the Prophet choosing a peaceful, as opposed to violent, option.

Choosing and abiding by the peaceful option, the Prophet carried on his preaching work for thirteen years in Mecca. Despite this, the Qureish fiercely opposed him, so much so that the Qureish elders plotted to kill him. Accordingly, they armed themselves with swords and surrounded his house. This was nothing short of a declaration of war against the Prophet and his companions. However, guided by God, the Prophet decided not to retaliate militarily, and in the darkness of night he left Mecca and travelled to Medina. This journey is known in Islam as the Hijrah. The hijrah exemplifies the choice of the use of the peaceful option, instead of a violent option.

The 'Battle of the Trench' is another example of the choice of the peaceful option by the Prophet. On this occasion, an army of the Prophet's opponents marched on Medina to attack the Prophet. This was an open declaration of war on their part. However, in order to avoid fighting, the Prophet arranged for a trench to be dug around the town. This served as a buffer against the attackers. Consequently, the Qureish army spent just a few days camped beyond the trench and then went back. Constructing the trench to keep off the invading Qureish was another example from the Prophet's life of choosing a peaceful, instead of violent, option.

Likewise, in the case of the Treaty of Hudaibiyah, the Prophet and his companions wanted to worship at Mecca, but they were stopped by the Qureish chiefs at a place called Hudaibiyah and were asked to go back to Medina. The Qureish said that they would not allow them to enter Mecca at any cost. This was, in a sense, a declaration of war on their part. If the Prophet had proceeded with his plans of proceeding to Mecca to worship, it would have meant armed conflict with the Qureish. However, the Prophet chose not to go ahead. Instead, he peacefully accepted a one-sided treaty with the Qureish and returned to Medina. This is yet another example of the Prophet choosing the peaceful, instead of violent, option.

This practice and preference was also evident when the Prophet finally took over Mecca. On this occasion, he was accompanied by ten thousand devoted companions, who could easily have militarily defeated the Qureish of Mecca. However, here, too, the Prophet did not use physical force to capture the

Origins of Jihad in the English Language

The *Webster* [Second Edition Dictionary] also gives us two good pieces of information [about the word jihad]. It tells us that the origin of the word *Jihad* is Arabic and it means struggle, strife. It also tells us that the word came into English usage during 1865–70. This period is the beginning of the popular struggle against the British in India as well as in Egypt and Sudan after the fall of their governments to the British. Notable among the new leaders is Mohammad Ahmed, the Mahdi [redeemer of Islam described in prophecies] of Sudan who waged a vigorous *Jihad* against the British to liberate Sudan (he is a celebrated villain in British and British-inspired history and the foe of the British hero 'Lord Gordon of Khartoom'). Thus the word *Jihad* comes into English usage at the time some Muslims were mobilizing under this slogan to expel the external conquerors.

Dr. Mohammed Shafi, "Jihad—Sacred Struggle,"
Dar al Islam Institute, *Alumni Newsletter, Fall 2003.*

town. Instead, he quietly travelled, along with his companions, to Mecca and entered it. This happened so suddenly that the Qureish were unable to make any preparations against them. Consequently, Mecca was won without any bloodshed. This, too, is an example of the choice of peaceful, instead of violent, means.

The Effectiveness of Peaceful Methods

These examples suggest that not just in ordinary situations, but also in situations of emergency, the Prophet resorted to peaceful, as opposed to violent, means. As indicated above, in Islam peace is the rule and war is the exception, and that too only when it becomes unavoidable. Keep this principle in mind and survey the world today. Today's world is very different from the world of ancient times, when war was the rule and was commonly resorted to. Choosing peaceful means was very difficult. However, today the situation has completely changed. In today's world, resort to violence has become completely useless and undesirable, while the use of peaceful means alone is generally accepted. So acceptable has the peaceful option become that it has emerged as a powerful force in its own right. Today, one can press one's views peacefully, through use of the right to free expression, using modern communications and the media. These developments have made the peaceful option even more efficacious.

As mentioned earlier, the Prophet's practice indicates that when peaceful options are available, they should be used and violent means should be abstained from. In today's context not only are peaceful methods and options available in plenty, but also, owing to various supporting factors, they are much more effective. It would not be an exaggeration to claim that in today's world violent methods have not only become more difficult, but also, in practical terms, completely useless. In contrast, peaceful methods are easier and also much more effective. Peaceful methods have now become the only possible and efficacious option. In this context one can claim that violent methods have to be abandoned, or what in the language of the shariah [Islamic law] is called 'mansukh' or abrogated. Now the followers of Islam have only one option to choose, and that, without any doubt, is the peaceful option, unless, of course conditions change so much that the directive needs to be changed.

It is true that in the past violent means were occasionally used but these were only under compulsion due to temporal factors. Now, because conditions have so changed that the compulsion no longer remains, the use of violent means is no longer necessary and is undesirable. Under the new conditions, only peaceful methods should be used. As far as the issue of jihad is concerned, peace is the rule and war has the status of only an unavoidable exception. . . .

According to a well-known principle of Islamic jurisprudence, rules change in the wake of change of time and place. This means that when the context changes one must seek to re-apply the juridical rule in accordance with and to suit the new context. This principle applies as much to issues of war as it does to other matters. This principle thus demands that violent methods be declared as abandoned and only peaceful methods should be given the status of being sanctioned by the shariah.

Jihad and Organized Government

Today, in various countries Muslims are involved in armed movements in the name of 'Islamic jihad'. However, simply by being called as a 'jihadi' movement by its leaders no such movement can be actually considered thus. No action can be considered as a legitimate jihad unless it fully meets the conditions as laid down in Islam. Those battles that are being fought in the name of jihad without meeting the conditions of jihad cannot be termed as jihad. Rather, they are fasad or strife [the opposite of jihad]. And those who are engaged in such activities will not get the reward [from God] of jihad. Instead, they will be considered worthy of punishment in God's eyes.

I have written extensively elsewhere about the various conditions necessary for qital or physical war to be truly considered as jihad. Here I wish to clarify just one point, and that is that jihad in the sense of qital is not a private act in the same manner as prayers and fasting. Rather, it is an act that is entirely associated with a state or government. This is clearly indicated in the Quran and the Hadith [reports attributed to or about the Prophet Muhammad]. For instance, the Quran says that in the face of intimidation by the enemy, individuals should not take any action on their own, but, instead, should turn to those in charge of their affairs so that the latter can understand the matter in a proper perspective and take appropriate and necessary steps. This means that individual members of the public cannot decide issues of war on their own. This is something left to the government to handle.

Likewise, a Hadith report states that the Imam or leader is like a shield, war is conducted under his control and through him safety is ensured. This means that war and defence must always be left to the rulers to manage. . . .

There is an almost unanimous opinion on this issue in the Islamic juridical tradition and almost no noted Islamic scholar has dissented from this. Hence, the [almost] unanimous opinion of the Islamic jurisprudents is that war can be declared only by an established government. Subjects or citizens of a state do not have the right to do so.[. . .] Today, in various places Muslims are engaged in fighting with governments in the name of jihad. However, almost without exception, these are not really Islamic jihads, but, rather, are fasad or condemnable strife. None of these so-called jihads has been declared by any government. All of these self-styled jihads have been declared and are conducted by non-state forces and actors. If some of these violent movements have the backing of any Muslim government, this is being done secretly, while according to the shariah, jihad on the part of a government must entail an open declaration. Without this, qital on the part of a Muslim government is illegal.

Today, the various violent movements in the name of jihad being engaged in by some Muslims are of two types: they are either guerrilla wars or proxy wars. Both sorts of war are completely illegal according to Islam. Guerrilla wars are unacceptable in Islam because they are led and conducted by non-state actors, not by any established government. Likewise, proxy wars are unacceptable in Islam because the governments behind them do not issue a formal and open declaration of war. This is not allowed in Islam.

Constructive and Continuous Jihad

Islamic jihad, properly understood, is a constructive and continuous process. It remains active throughout the life of a true believer. It has three aspects:

1. Jihad-e nafs, or the struggle against the baser self or the ego, against one's passions and wrong desires and to remain steadfast in one's commitment to lead the life that God wants for human beings.

2. Jihad in the sense of striving, using peaceful means, to communicate God's word to all of His slaves, inspired by a compassion and concern for others, even if this is not reciprocated. This is the great jihad according to the Quran.

3. The third form of jihad relates to confronting one's foes and to remain firmly committed to the faith under all conditions. In the past, this form of jihad . . . was basically a peaceful action, and so remains even today. In this sense, jihad, properly understood, is a peaceful struggle, not military or physical confrontation.

> "We must constantly reassure our moderate Muslim friends . . . that we are at war with all terrorists, not all Muslims."

Demonizing Islam Is Wrong and Foolish

Richard Warren Field

Richard Warren Field argues in the following viewpoint that Islam as a religion is no more violent than other major world religions such as Christianity and Judaism. Furthermore, he states that by demonizing an entire religion, moderates within said religion are alienated and end up siding with extremists to fend off unjust attacks. Finally, Field examines the contributions Muslims have made to Western society and encourages Westerners to reach out to moderate Muslims for support in the war against terrorists. Field is the author of the novels The Election *and* The Swords of Faith.

As you read, consider the following questions:

1. What are some of the incidents of violence identified by the author as having been perpetrated by the followers of religions such as Christianity and Judaism?

Richard Warren Field, "Demonizing Islam Is Both Wrong and Foolish," RichardWarren Field.com, May 30, 2006, updated on January 26, 2009. Reproduced by permission.

2. According to the author, why are many moderate Muslims silent when it comes to speaking out against the actions of Islamic extremists?

3. What contributions does the author state Muslims have made to Western civilization?

Almost immediately after Nine-Eleven, President Bush clearly and adamantly stated that the United States would not be fighting a war against Islam. We were to fight individuals and groups who perpetrate terrorism and have misappropriated Islam. That was one of the wisest policies of his leadership. I have heard political commentators and religious leaders, some of whom I agree with on many other issues, make vehement arguments that Islam itself, as a religious faith, is the problem. They say Islam is not a religion of peace, but incites the violence and intolerance we see in our enemies in the war on terror. If Islam itself really is the enemy, then are we fighting a billion people? This would put us at war for the foreseeable future, a depressing prospect. But fortunately, Islam itself isn't the problem. So demonizing Islam is both foolish and counter-productive.

Violence in Christianity and Judaism

People who want to demonize Islam per se as our enemy refer to two main sources for their arguments—quotations from Islamic scriptures, and the lack of a serious protest by moderate Muslims against the hijacking of their religion by radical reactionary Muslims.

On the scripture issue, I am simply not qualified to make expert comments on the scriptures of Islam. My own background is Christian, and I wouldn't even pretend to be an expert in Christian scripture. I do know that religious scriptures can be misquoted, quoted out of context, mistranslated and misinterpreted. There are virulent anti-Jewish scriptures in the Christian New Testament. But at the time these scriptures were written, the religious group that would become the Christian establishment generations later was involved in fierce clashes with established Jewish sects. These passages in Christian scriptures were written as counter-attacks against that repression. Christianity was not the dominant religion at the time of these scriptures. It was a religion threatened with extinction. Sadly, Christian anti-Semitism sprang from a literal interpretation of these scriptures, taken out of their historical context, and that anti-Semitism was a shameful element of the Christian past. But no reasonable person would label current Christianity, which almost universally rejects anti-Semitism, as a violent and bigoted religion based on those scriptures.

Jewish scriptures also describe violent actions against the enemies of the Jewish people. These scriptures were also created at a time when the Jewish people were struggling for survival against powerful and ruthless neighbors. Some anti-Israel rhetoric has attempted to use quotes from Jewish scriptures to prove Judaism is a violent religion, and therefore that Israel is a violent nation. But the idea that Judaism today is an inherently violent religion is not well-documented or widely accepted.

Violence with Compassion and Justice

Islam faced its own enemies during Mohammed's lifetime. Mohammed addressed the proper conduct of battles with those enemies, and mandated the merciful treatment of captured prisoners, and the prohibition against causing harm to innocent non-combatants. (This aspect of Islam has been completely disregarded by the Muslim terrorists today. Or, they have found a way to rationalize their behavior by labeling all non-Muslims as legitimate combatants?) Just the fact that Mohammed addressed these issues might imply that Islam is an inherently violent religion. But we must understand that Mohammed and his followers faced destruction by enemy military forces while Mohammed was alive. Mohammed made the choice to defend himself and his followers. The military activities undertaken were defensive.

Those arguing that Christianity is a more peaceful religion will point out that if Jesus had faced similar challenges, he might have counseled his followers to turn the other cheek. Jesus offered his followers a spiritual answer for his times. His community was almost completely disempowered. Those who chose to fight the Roman authorities met horrendous fates. So Jesus offered them a spiritual approach that would allow them to lead meaningful lives in the midst of a hopeless earthly situation. (Jesus was also capable of some violence when faced with injustices directed against his followers—his encounter with the money-changers in the Jerusalem temple during the week before his death verifies this point.) In Mohammed's time, he and his followers were not so disempowered. They had the ability to resist their persecutors. If Mohammed's followers had turned the other cheek, they would probably have been slaughtered. So Mohammed set rules for fighting for an earthly existence, with compassion and justice.

The Problems of Moderate Muslims

In addressing the issue of Islam itself as a cause of the current hostilities with Muslim terrorists, it is more important to examine how Muslims practice their religion in the present day, than it is to try to assess the religion based on excerpts from scriptures prone to distortion when removed from their historical and rhetorical context. There is no doubt that the terrorist version of Islam does inspire hostilities. But what about the moderate Muslims? If their religion has truly been hijacked, then why haven't we heard from them? Why aren't they expressing their outrage and fighting for the soul of their religion? There is an obvious answer. They are afraid of the terrorists! The moderate Muslims are generally not violent people. They have every reason to fear that if they label the Muslim terrorist fanatics as operating outside the true tenets

Reporting the History of U.S.–Muslim Relations

The American public, and American journalists acting on its behalf in reporting on the Arab and Muslim worlds, must understand that the history of U.S. policy and intervention in these regions—from the beginning of the Cold War until today—is intimately connected to how Muslims throughout the world regard and react to us. We need to understand that these policies are carried out in our name and they shape Muslim perceptions not only of our government, but also of us (as citizens who freely elect it). Toward this end, the journalism must not only give voice to Muslim attitudes but also probe and contextualize historical and political facts upon which they are based.

Without this perspective, the reporting will remain incomplete and along with it Americans' understanding of a part of the world that is increasingly tied to our own interests and well being.

Marda Dunsky,
"Reporting the Arab and Muslim Worlds,"
Nieman Reports, *Summer 2007.*

of Islam, then they will become the targets of terrorist wrath. In fact, they would be more of a threat to the terrorists, because their opposition would threaten the very legitimacy of the terrorists' existence.

Or, moderate Muslims may still be assessing where they belong in this struggle. In his book *No God But God*, Reza Aslan asserts that Islam is involved in nothing less than a civil war. Moderates are fighting with extremists for the soul of the religion. If this is true, then when Christians, or other westerners, demonize Islam, and not the misappropriation of it, they back those moderates into a corner, compelling them to make a choice between fanatics in their own religion and those who condemn their religion itself as the enemy. We are helping the extremist Muslims by pushing the moderates into their camp if we attack a religion with over a billion followers on the planet.

Historical Contributions and the Destruction of Islam

We should not demonize Islam, but reach out to the moderate Muslims. We need to let them know we understand and respect the contributions of Islam to our civilization. From the 700s to the 1200s, Muslim scholars preserved western knowledge while Europe was enveloped in the "Dark Ages." Large numbers of manuscripts of the pre-Christian Greek civilization were translated into Arabic. The knowledge was then improved upon in various disciplines, including astronomy, mathematics, and medicine. The advanced civilization during that period was the Muslim civilization, stretching from Central Asia to Spain. Non-Muslim scholars also participated in this Muslim golden age, treated with the most religious tolerance offered by any state in existence at that time.

Islam then underwent an assault from two directions. The Crusades, from the west, placed stresses on a politically fragmenting Muslim world. The Mongols from the east then threatened the very existence of Islam, destroying much of the Muslim Central Asian civilization. Mongols moved toward the heartland of Islam, destroying Baghdad, the grand city of Islam's golden age. Islam has never completely recovered from the Mongol conquests. Merv was the most populated city in the world during the middle of the 12th Century, its prosperity driven by a thriving trade over the Silk Route. The city was larger than Constantinople, larger than Baghdad, and much larger than Paris or London. The Mongols obliterated the city.

Remnants of the city survive today, as curiosities for archaeologists. The Mongols significantly depopulated Central Asia, destroying entire cities in the process. Baghdad was subjected to a wholesale slaughter of anyone not considered useful to the Mongols. They reduced the city from a spiritual capital of Islam to a provincial town. The city struggled for centuries to regain some of the glories of the its golden age. Western Europe, spared from the Mongol cataclysm, emerged from the wreckage to make use of the preserved Greek knowledge, and other Muslim innovations in medicine (including hospitals) and mathematics (including Arabic numbers, though they may have originated in India). Islam was the religion of progress before the Mongol cataclysm. Let's acknowledge our debt to Islam, and invite Muslims to join in the continuing progress of humanity.

We also hear the argument "if you want to see what true Islam is, just look at the situation in Saudi Arabia." This simply isn't true. Yes, Saudi Arabia currently rules over the area of Islam's most sacred shrines. But their sect of Islam should not be considered as some sort of Muslim orthodoxy. As Reza Aslan also points out in his book *No God But God*, it is through an accident of history that the obscure Wahhabi sect, originally conceived by Abd al-Wahhab during the Eighteenth Century, came to prominence. Wahabi Islam began as a reactionary approach to Islam. It might well be compared to the Puritanism of England in the 1600s. Wahabi Islam might have faded off onto the margins of the religion if it hadn't been embraced by a tribal leader, Muhammad ibn Saud, whose descendants ended up possessing one of the largest oil reserves on the planet. We need to understand that the Islam of Saudi Arabia is not the Islam practiced by all one billion plus Muslims. When we condemn the abuses and injustices of Wahabi Islam, the same sort of Islam that gave rise to the Taliban, we need to make sure it is clear we understand this form of Islam is not followed by all Muslims.

A Coalition Against Radical Islam

It is a sad fact that all the major religions seem to lapse into factions at some point. Great spiritual leaders come along with insights that inspire humanity. But after those spiritual visionaries pass on, their legacies are entrusted to mere ordinary people, who end up distorting and even losing the vision. Jesus would certainly have wept at the atrocities committed in his name. Mohammed would most certainly be disgusted with the terrorists invoking his name as they send men, women and sometimes even children out to destroy innocent people with suicidal bomb attacks. It is important for non-Muslims to reach out to the less radical Muslims with understanding, and ask them to stand with us against the radical Muslims who will go so far to restore some idealized vision of past Islamic glory that they would destroy the present. Our President's initial statements about Islam were correct. We must constantly reassure our moderate Muslim friends, and those Muslims still torn between radical and moderate Islam, that we are at war with all terrorists, not all Muslims.

> *"By talking about Islamic terrorism as a monolith, we have fallen for Bin Laden's tricks, and risk pushing many terrorist groups with different agendas closer together."*

All Islamic Terrorists Are Not the Same

Justine A. Rosenthal

In the viewpoint that follows, Justine A. Rosenthal distinguishes the differences between nationalistically motivated terrorist groups that may have Islam as their religion and religiously motivated terrorist groups that justify their actions with scripture. She argues that by grouping nationalistic and Islamic terrorists into one group, the United States and its allies risk pushing groups with markedly different goals together. Specifically, she worries that unless U.S. rhetoric and policy does not differentiate between the two motivations, groups such as Hamas and Hizballah, which were formed to achieve nationalistic goals, will join forces with terrorists such as al-Qaeda that seek to establish a

Justine A. Rosenthal, "Jigsaw Jihadism," *National Interest*, vol. 87, January 2007, pp. 61-66. Copyright © 2007 *National Interest*, Washington, D.C. Reproduced by permission.

global Islamic state. Rosenthal is the executive editor of National Interest *and researched terrorism issues as a fellow in foreign policy studies at the Brookings Institution, a public policy think tank.*

As you read, consider the following questions:

1. What does Rosenthal believe to be the two dangers in thinking of the war against terrorism as "an all-or-nothing war"?
2. What are some of the terrorist organizations Rosenthal worries are expanding and beginning to pursue the Islamic agenda of al-Qaeda?
3. What two strategies does Rosenthal suggest to combat the teaming up of nationalistic terrorists with al-Qaeda?

Lately, all terrorism seems to be about Islam, and it all seems to be the same. A snapshot: turn on CNN to watch a gruesome play-by-play of our War on Terror, scan the best-seller list for the newest book on Osama bin Laden, leaf through the newspaper to see the latest suicide terror attack. By all accounts the specter of jihadism looms large. Yet, some unintended trickery is afoot—imagery making the threat to Western democracy, which is frightening enough, seem like the worst kind of Hollywood doomsday movie.

Grouping All Terrorist Groups Together Is Wrong

Even if we suspend belief for a moment and simply cast aside all those terrorist groups that clearly have nothing at all to do with the Islamic religion—the Tamil Tigers in Sri Lanka, the FARC [Revolutionary Armed Forces of Columbia] in Colombia and the IRA [Irish Republican Army] in Ireland (to name but a few)—we are still left with a slew of seemingly similar groups all motivated by and distorting Islam to suit their own ends. Yet the problem is far more complex and, as we disaggregate the threat, we see that although "Islamic terrorism" prevails in many cases, the goals of these terrorist groups are often strikingly different.

Even if all of these terrorists intone various distortions of the Islamic religion, there are no universal agendas. The goal for groups like Hamas, Palestinian Islamic Jihad and the Chechen rebels is "a nation of their own" with tactics reminiscent of the ethnic violence erupting after abandoned colonialism. Groups with traditional nation-state aims—even if they use Islamic rhetoric—have little interest, if any, in the United States. Their goals remain narrow and less fearsome.

On the other end of the spectrum are groups like Jemaah Islamiya (JI) and Al-Qaeda with its various offshoots, who indeed are looking to rearrange the global order, instigate the now-infamous clash of civilizations and create a Muslim caliphate that spans continents, all the while bringing the West to its knees. Their goals are vast and global. Somewhere in the middle of all this are groups at risk, Lashkar-e-Taiba (LET) in Pakistan and the separatist movements in the Philippines and Thailand. These groups are primarily motivated by state-centric goals, but all rest on the cusp of pan-territorial and far more dangerous agendas.

Without doubt, the United States needs to counter Islamic terrorists seeking the ascendance of an Islamic caliphate and the concomitant destruction of the West. But this is not a battle against all terrorists in which the Islamic religion plays a role. The danger in thinking about it as an all-or-nothing war is two-fold: first, that we will miscategorize these state-centered groups and so create inappropriate counter-terrorism strategies; second, that by doing so we will push groups that have constrained goals toward the pan-global agenda of Al-Qaeda—creating the very threat we fear most.

Distinguishing Between Nationalist and Religious Terrorists

There is no massive monolith hurtling toward us, razing everything in its path. There are a few big boulders and a whole lot of pebbles. Which direction and how much momentum they take on may be mainly up to us. Terrorist groups can largely be conceived as having two working parts: an identity and an ideology. When it comes to Islamic terrorism, that identity is based in religion, but sometimes the ideology is based in nationalism, while at other times in a more ephemeral, pan-territorial agenda. This difference is most stark between more traditional "ethno-terrorist" movements and the far more globally oriented groups like Al-Qaeda. As Al-Qaeda's top strategist Ayman al-Zawahiri makes clear, there is a significant difference between Islamic national liberation movements and those struggling for a new Islamic global order:

> Many of the liberation battles in our Muslim world had used composite slogans that mixed nationalism with Islam and, indeed, sometimes caused Islam to intermingle with leftist, communist slogans. . . . The Palestinian issue is the best example of these intermingled slogans and beliefs under the influence of an idea of allying oneself with the devil for the sake of liberating Palestine. They allied themselves with the devil, but lost Palestine.

Recent statements by Hamas leaders draw a virtually identical distinction. Mahmoud Zahar, now Hamas's foreign minister, once put it this way:

> Al-Qaeda is not present here. We are focused on the occupation. We run no operations outside of Palestine, outside of the occupied territories, so we are completely different from Al-Qaeda.

These differences do go beyond mere rhetoric. It is almost impossible to take terrorists' statements at face value, but when those in Hamas argue that their violent acts are poles apart from those of Al-Qaeda they are telling the truth. It is also evident in deed.

National versus Global Targets

Since nationalist movements are focused on creating a state or political freedoms for one group, their strategies are focused on the nation-state from which they hope to gain concessions. Their violence is directed at those inside the state. Whether or not Islam provides the identity, their goals are not apocalyptic. In contrast, religious terrorist groups like Al-Qaeda engage in almost no domestic targeting. Their goals cross continents. They want to destroy corrupt regimes in the Middle East, South and Southeast Asia, purge the Western presence in their lands and change the global power order. This is why the bombers in Bali attack Marriott hotels, foreign nightclubs and beach resorts. When a file was found on a computer of one of the planners of the October 2005 Bali bombings, the instructions and strategies laid bare on these virtual pages were pretty disturbing. Amongst the minutiae of what clothing to wear to blend in with the crowds, and the size of the bombs and backpacks, was the larger thinking about targets. The attacks were aimed at Westerners, specifically foreign tourists. Since it would be hard to figure out where people were from, they simply decided that "all white people [are] the enemy." Even the locations they scouted were Western: McDonald's, Pizza Hut, Burger King. All the other attacks by Jemaah Islamiya [JI] were no different. Every one has been aimed at an international target with foreign civilian occupants: the Kuta and Jimbaran tourist areas in Bali, the Australian Embassy in Jakarta and the Hilton hotel in the Egyptian resort town of Taba. As a JI suspect held in the 2002 Bali bombings explained, once an Islamic state in Indonesia was achieved, members would work toward a larger daulah islamiyah nusantara encompassing Malaysia, Indonesia, Thailand, Singapore and the Philippines, and then move on to restoring the Islamic caliphate.

There remain very different forms of Islamic terrorism: traditional struggles for political freedom for an ethnic group trapped in a nation-state run by an "other", and battles to rework the global order, join a communal group across continents and bring down the prevailing culture. These types of Islamic terrorist groups behave differently, pose different threat levels to the United States and require divergent counterterrorism strategies because they have dissimilar goals.

Pushing Nationalist Groups Toward Al-Qaeda

Only slightly less frightening than Islamic terrorism itself is our incorrect understanding of exactly what is going on, and the inappropriate and potentially counterproductive policies ensuing from our misinterpretations. Initially, no one, including the [George W. Bush] administration, thought Hamas or the Chechens or any other Islamic terrorist group had anything to do with Al-Qaeda. But, by talking about Islamic terrorism as a monolith, we have fallen for Bin Laden's tricks, and risk pushing many terrorist groups with different agendas closer together.

As Bin Laden's rhetoric becomes increasingly pervasive and persuasive, something quite dangerous is happening. Though there has been much talk of the growth of "self-starter" cells—groups of Al-Qaeda adherents with no actual connection to the central command—it is the established local groups with state-centric agendas we also need to be ever-more concerned about. These groups are evolving and their goals are expanding. Most dangerous, their capabilities and infrastructure are already in place. The merger of Zawahiri's Egyptian Islamic Jihad and Al-Qaeda in 1998 led to one of the deadliest terrorist movements the world has ever known. If

The Ideological Differences Between Hamas and Al-Qaida

There are numerous fundamental ideological and political differences between Hamas and al-Qaida, which the typical Western reader knows very little about. Ideologically, Hamas has adopted and promotes the relatively moderate school of thought espoused by Harakat al-Ikhwan al Muslimun—the Muslim Brotherhood—which advocates peaceful means, not violence, in effecting change in Islamic societies. In contrast, Al-Qaida adopts a school of thought called "Madrasat al Fikr al Salafi al Jihadi" or the "School of the fighting-Salafi ideology," a program quite at odds with that adopted by Muslim Brotherhood organizations like Hamas. . . .

Hamas believes in the comprehensiveness of the application of Islam in all walks of life—in a person's belief system, and in a society's politics, economy, education, law, the arts, and the media. The belief in the "comprehensiveness of the application of Islam in all walks of life" is what the Muslim Brothers in Palestine and elsewhere in the Arab world have been preaching and attempting to apply for decades, with varying degrees of success. That program stands in stark contradistinction from the program al-Qaida, which has adopted a program of armed Jihad as its sole mode of operation. Al-Qaida pays little or no attention the idea of reforming societies from within and eschews the effectiveness of transforming societies through peaceful means.

Khalid Amayreh, "Hamas and al-Qaida: The Prospects for Radicalization in the Palestinian Occupied Territories," Conflicts Forum: Beirut-London-Washington, October 2007.

more local groups join ranks in this larger global struggle, the potential for destruction is almost unfathomable. And these local groups are coming together, turning more lethal and looking more like Al-Qaeda everyday. In December 2004, the Abu Sayyaf Group, yet another Filipino separatist movement, cooperated with Jemaah Islamiya to bomb the General Santos City public market, killing 15 and injuring 58. Hizballah and Hamas colluded in the recent war in southern Lebanon and the LET [Lashkar-e-Toiba, South Asian Islamic Organization], once a worry only in Kashmir [a disputed region on the Indian subcontinent], is becoming increasingly dangerous, reportedly recently responsible for injuring 625 people in the Mumbai [India] transit bombings. They are even sprouting cells in Virginia.

Making matters worse, the Algerian Salafist Group for Call and Combat (GSPC), thought to be primarily concerned with making Algeria an Islamist state, proclaimed allegiance to Al-Qaeda in September [2006], stating it considers itself "one stone in building the coming Islamic nation." Growing unrest in Thailand, Cambodia and Malaysia, and the potential for various Filipino groups to place nationalistic agendas on the back burner in favor of Al-Qaeda's larger Islamic struggle is alarming. Groups keep falling into Al-Qaeda's clutches.

Understanding the Motivations of Nationalist Terrorists

Ethnic terrorist groups like Hamas have a tendency to endure because they represent a distinct ethnic "other" with a clear and constrained political agenda. This kind of deep-seated ethnic terrorism only ends with viable political solutions. The state needs to plow through negotiations and keep on track no matter the level of terrorism, while avoiding extreme retaliatory policies. This is evidenced by the sometimes successful Sri Lankan peace process and the cessation of violence in Ireland. The Israeli and Spanish policies of "going it alone" worked in part because they moved ahead with peace programs in spite of spoilers, infighting and competition for power. Violent crackdowns and knee-jerk derailments always fail.

Ethnic terrorists are the oppressed minority's proxy. So, when the groups go too far, lost public support reins them in. Conversely, harsh government measures increase support for terrorism because the sense of oppression is reinforced. Palestinian belief in the need for violence was at its lowest right before the second intifada, but increased as Israel cracked down. The West Bank and Gaza Strip closures created a massive humanitarian crisis. Rather than lessening public support for terrorism, Israeli retaliation added to the animosity—the terrorists were not viewed as the cause of suffering, the government of Israel was. Support for terrorism only ebbed at the end of Israel's Operation Protective Shield in April of 2002. The cycle of violence depends on the behaviors of both parties.

Yes, Al-Qaeda shares "Islamic identity" with groups like Hamas—but not the same sort of political agenda. Groups with nationalistic goals tend to have sea legs; groups with more ephemeral agendas tend to peter out over time. The left-wing movements which wreaked such havoc in Europe during the 1970s and 1980s were destroyed by a disintegrating agenda. The less viable communism looked, the less public support for the "red terrorists." So, one of the main strengths of religious terrorism is also a point of great potential vulnerability. Its pan-territorial appeal makes it possible to tap into the extremist populations of many states, allowing for multiple bases, diverse cells and a large recruitment pool. But, national identity can trump religious affiliation. Primordial urges are strong. And if the nationalist agenda looks achievable, the impetus to fight for a larger religious one fades.

Ideology Supports Terrorism

Most of the groups that now cooperate with Al-Qaeda began with a primarily nationalistic agenda. By differentiating between groups with goals of statehood or political enfranchisement that use religion as the communal identity versus groups with aspirations of a religious global struggle, we take the first steps to creating enmity among extremists.

This leaves us with two strategies. The first is to get state-centric terrorist groups back to the negotiating table in an effort to reinforce their nationalist impulses and lessen the attraction of forming a common front with Al-Qaeda. The second is to engage full-force in the battle over ideology central to destroying the appeal and spread of Al-Qaeda over the longer term.

Right now, there is a dearth of competing ideologies. Throughout the Islamic world, religious extremists have a monopoly in the marketplace of ideas. We need to hasten an eclipse of this ideological historical moment because when an ideology fails, the terrorism that sprang from it dies too.

There remains little agreement and great debate over the root causes of religious terrorism. How much education, religious doctrine, the current global political order, poverty and a variety of other variables play a role in creating religious terrorism is unclear. We are unlikely ever to get to the bottom of all of these questions. . . .

Ending Terrorism by Recognizing Differences in Goals

This is a battle for ideological dominance, and one part of the struggle against religious terrorism in the fight against membership in the larger Al-Qaeda schema. The global religious terrorists' multinational appeal and dogmatic ties are frightening enough. The idea that every group bound by some form of Muslim religious tenet is ipso facto a part of Al-Qaeda needlessly complicates our efforts. Hamas, the PFLP [Popular

Front for the Liberation of Palestine], Chechen rebels and the like remain state-centric terrorists, more concerned with strict territorial goals than with the larger Islamic struggle. They are a separate threat, and less of a problem for the world as a whole. But if they are categorized as a part of the larger battle against religious terrorism and swooped up in the net of aggressive U.S. policies, this would likely have the inverse of the intended effect—bringing these groups and their goals closer to those of Al-Qaeda rather than further away.

The political demands of religious terrorists are non-negotiable. Unlike ethnic terrorists, for whom peace will inevitably be tied to real political reform, religious terrorists' goals are too vast and too amorphous for negotiation. The desire to change the global power hierarchy creates an untenable situation. This is why a competing ideology must be addressed: an ideology that can appeal to the same audience, address the same inequities, but one which does not promote a distorted, violent global jihad.

It is our only way out.

Periodical Bibliography

The following articles have been selected to supplement the diverse views presented in this chapter.

J. Keith Akins	"A Broader Conceptualization of Islam and Terrorism," *JFQ: Joint Force Quarterly*, Spring 2007.
Karen Armstrong	"The True, Peaceful Face of Islam," *Time*, September 23, 2001.
Tom Flynn	"Islamofacism: Fiction or Threat?" *Free Inquiry*, August-September 2008.
Fawaz A. Gerges	"Understanding the Many Faces of Islamism and Jihadism," *Nieman Reports*, Summer 2007.
Mathias Kuntzel	"Suicide Terrorism and Islam," *American Foreign Policy Interests*, July-August 2008.
Hal Lindsey	"Islam's Violent Core," WorldNetDaily, June 24, 2004. www.wnd.com.
Mohammed Omer	"'In the Name of Islam': Reality or Excuse?" *Washington Report on Middle East Affairs*, July 2007.
Marc Sageman	"The Reality of Grass-Roots Terrorism," *Foreign Affairs*, July-August 2008.
Robert Spencer	"No Jihadis Here!" *Human Events*, April 5, 2008.
Mark Steyn	"Denial Is a River in Washington, and London," *National Review*, July 30, 2007.
Amir Taheri	"What Do Muslims Think?" *American Interest*, May-June 2007.
Michael Ware	"Meet the New Jihad," *Time*, July 5, 2004.

CHAPTER 3

What Is the Status of Women Under Islam?

Chapter Preface

On July 6, 2008, in Jonesboro, Georgia, a fifty-four-year-old Pakistani immigrant, Chaudhry Rashid, allegedly killed his twenty-five-year-old daughter Sandella Kanwal. The case has been dubbed by the U.S. media as an "honor killing" because the offender and victim were both Muslim and because Kanwal was seeking to dissolve the marriage her father had arranged for her.

In 2002, Sandella Kanwal submitted to an arranged marriage to a Pakistani man named Majid Latif. Upon returning to the United States, Kanwal lived with her husband for several years. In April 2008, the couple separated, and on July 1, 2008, Sandella Kanwal filed for divorce. On July 6, 2008, Kanwal and her father argued. He was angered she wanted to leave her husband. At the close of the argument, Chaudhry Rashid allegedly entered his daughter's bedroom and strangled her to death.

Rashid admitted in court to killing his daughter. At his arraignment, Rashid stated (through his translator), "I have done nothing wrong." This admission led journalists to the conclusion Rashid had killed his daughter because of the shame she supposedly brought upon the family name by ending her marriage. Such dishonor is the motivation associated with so-called honor killings, a practice assumed to be legitimate and not uncommon in Muslim communities worldwide.

Some commentators argued Rashid's actions were irredeemable but had little to do with being Muslim. Ajay Nair, associate dean of multicultural affairs at Columbia University, told CNN that such killings were not isolated to South Asian communities; rather the true tragedy is that "domestic violence . . . cuts across all communities." He asserted it is a human rights issue that needs to be addressed to protect women.

Robert Spencer, the director of the Jihad Watch Web site, counters that view, stating that spokespersons like Nair are simply apologists for a type of crime that is intimately tied to Islam. On Jihad Watch, Spencer asserts that "the price of this politically correct refusal to confront the ugly realities of the Islamic link to honor killing will be, quite simply, more honor killings." Spencer is one of the authors who, in the following chapter, debate whether women are victims of oppression under Islamic law.

> *"Islamic gender apartheid goes far beyond second class citizenship. It is intended to crush and subordinate women."*

Islam Oppresses Women

Robert Spencer and Phyllis Chesler

Robert Spencer is the director of Jihad Watch, a program of the David Horowitz Freedom Center, and the author of eight books on Islam and jihad. He is also a weekly columnist for Human Events *and* FrontPage Magazine. *Phyllis Chesler is a writer, psychotherapist, and professor of psychology and women's studies at the College of Staten Island. In the following viewpoint, Spencer and Chesler argue that through practices such as female circumcision, veiling, rape, and beatings, Islamic women are being physically and mentally oppressed. The authors contend that while these acts are not condoned by Islamic law or the Koran, Islamic society has created an environment where these acts are the accepted norm.*

As you read, consider the following questions:

1. According to Spencer and Chesler, why did the Prophet Muhammad give permission to men to beat their wives?

2. As the authors explain, how are Muslim men able to obtain easy divorces?

3. In the authors' opinion, why is it nearly impossible to prove rape in lands that follow *sharia* law?

[T]he] facts show that the war we're fighting isn't just about bombs and hijacked airliners. It's also about the oppression of women—often in horrific ways. Nor is this oppression an incidental byproduct of terrorism. The Islamic law—*Sharia*—that terrorists are fighting to impose upon the world mandates institutionalized discrimination against women. Islamic gender apartheid goes far beyond second class citizenship. It is intended to crush and subordinate women.

In Afghanistan, images of women wearing stifling burqas, long gowns that cover their heads, faces, and bodies and seriously limit and impair their vision, became symbolic of life under the Taliban. That radical Muslim regime forbade women to be educated, or even to venture outdoors unaccompanied. Its "Morality" or "Vice and Virtue" police beat them with sticks in the street for trivial offenses. The oppression of women was at the very core of their government and their worldview. And other *jihad* terrorists want to impose a Taliban-style regime wherever they gain power.

Arab Women Are Prisoners

For Americans living in a world committed to equality between the sexes, it may seem hard to imagine that such systematic violence against women, sanctioned by religious belief, still exists. Yet across the Muslim world, women endure restrictions on their movements, their marital options, their professional opportunities, and more. In Kuwait, Saudi Arabia, and elsewhere, women cannot vote or hold office. According to Amnesty International, in Saudi Arabia "women . . . who walk unaccompanied, or are in the company of a man who is neither their husband nor a close relative, are at risk of arrest on suspicion of prostitution or other 'moral' offences." Nor is the oppression of women in Muslim lands some momentary accident of history. According to Saudi feminist Wajeha Al-Huwaider, the lives of many Arab women are similar to those of prisoners. However, the Arab woman is a prisoner in her own home, has committed no crime, was not captured in battle, does not belong to any terrorist army. According to Iranian exile Freidoune Sahebjam, the author of *The Stoning of Soraya M*, the Islamic woman's sin is having been born female, which constitutes a "capital offense" in an era of *jihad*.

Men have used the Koran and Islamic tradition and law systematically to create what Egyptian Muslim women's advocate Dr. Nawal El-Saadawi calls "a patriarchal class system in which males dominate females." The presumption, as the Koran says, that "men have a status above women" is pervasive in the Islamic world. And pressure on women to submit to this situation has been present since the founding of Islam. Aisha, the most beloved of the Muslim prophet Muhammad's many wives, admonished women in no uncertain terms to submit: "O womenfolk, if you knew the rights that your husbands have over you, every one of you would wipe the dust from her husband's feet with her face."

The oppression of women sanctioned by the teachings of Islam, and often by its holy book, manifests itself in innumerable ways. Here are some of the most notorious:

Female Circumcision

In some Islamic countries women face the certainty of female circumcision. Somali women's rights activist and ex-Muslim Ayaan Hirsi Ali notes that in her own homeland virtually every girl has her clitoris excised, sometimes when as young as five years old, and that the practice is always justified in the name of Islam. Uncircumcised girls are told they will become prostitutes but that circumcised girls will be pure. . . .

"Women in Islam." Cartoon by Kjell Nilsson-Maki. www.CartoonStock.com.

Genital mutilation is not a specifically Islamic custom. It is also practiced by a number of cultural and religious groups in Africa and South Asia. Among Muslims it's prevalent mainly in Egypt, Sudan, and Somalia, and in other African countries.

Yet despite the fact that there is scant affirmation in Islamic teaching for this horrific practice, the Muslims who do practice it invest genital mutilation with religious significance. One Islamic legal manual states that circumcision is required "for both men and women." . . .

Physical Beatings

The Pakistan Institute of Medical Sciences has determined that over ninety percent of Pakistani wives have been struck, beaten, or abused sexually—for offenses on the order of cooking an unsatisfactory meal or failing to give birth to a male child. Dominating their women by violence is a prerogative Muslim men cling to tenaciously. In Spring 2005, when the East African nation of Chad tried to institute a new family law that would outlaw wife beating, Muslim clerics led resistance to the measure as un-Islamic. Daughter-beating and sister-beating is just as routine as wife-beating and psychologically "seasons" girls to accept such treatment when they are grown.

Why do things like this happen?

Because Islamic clerics worldwide have spoken approvingly of the physical abuse of women. . . .

Why do they say such things?

Because the permission to beat one's wife is rooted in the Islamic holy book, the Koran, and Islamic tradition.

The Koran says: "Men shall take full care of women with the bounties which God has bestowed more abundantly on the former than on the latter, and with what they may spend out of their possessions. And the righteous women are the truly devout ones, who guard the intimacy which God has [ordained to be] guarded. And as for those women whose ill-will you have reason to fear, admonish them [first]; then leave them alone in bed; then beat them . . ."

Once told that "women have become emboldened towards their husbands," the prophet Muhammad "gave permission to beat them." He was unhappy with the women who complained, not with their husbands who committed acts of violence.

Muhammad even struck his favorite wife, Aisha. When he went out one night, Aisha surreptitiously followed him. When he found out what she had done, as she later said, "He struck me on the chest which caused me pain, and then said: Did you think that Allah and His Apostle would deal unjustly with you?"

Easy Divorce and Polygamy

A tragic house fire in March 2007 that killed a woman and nine children in a Bronx row house brought to light the practice of Islamic polygamy in the United States. Moussa Magassa, the owner of the house and father of five of the children who were killed, had two wives (both of whom survived the fire). The *New York Times* reported that "immigration to New York and other American cities has soared from places where polygamy is lawful and widespread, especially from West African countries like Mali, where demographic surveys show that 43 percent of women are in polygamous marriages."

Polygamy—which dehumanizes women and reduces them to the status of commodities, and which has long been outlawed in the United States—becomes part of these immigrants' new lives in the West. . . .

If polygamy is rooted in the Islamic holy book ("If ye fear that ye shall not be able to deal justly with the orphans, marry women of your choice, two or three or four . . .") so too is divorce. A Muslim man is able to divorce any of his wives simply by saying "I divorce you" or "You are divorced." The Koran stipulates only that a man wait for a suitable interval in order to make sure that his wife is not pregnant. If the divorcing couple has any children, they ordinarily go with the father, and he owes his wife no financial or any other kind of support. . . .

Veiling Women in Inequality

In February 2007, Zilla Huma Usman, the Pakistani government's minister for social welfare in Punjab province, was shot dead by a Muslim because her head was uncovered. The murderer, Mohammad Sarwar, declared: "I have no regrets. I just obeyed Allah's commandment. I will kill all those women who do not follow the right path, if I am freed again." In Algeria, "as in Iran, unveiled, educated, independent Algerian women have been seen as military targets and increasingly shot on sight." Attorney Karima Bennoune says: "The men of Algeria are arming, the women of Algeria are veiling themselves. As one woman said: 'Fear is stronger than our will to be free.'" In the Muslim holy city of Mecca in March 2002, fifteen teenage girls perished in a fire at their school when the Saudi religious police, the *muttawa* wouldn't let them out of the building. Why? Because in the female-only school environment, they had shed the all-concealing outer garments that Saudi women must wear in the presence of men. They had not put these garments back on before trying to flee from the fire. The *muttawa* preferred that they die rather than transgress Islamic law, actually battled police and firemen who were trying to open the school's doors and to save the girls. Because of such thinking, all across the Muslim world women endure restrictions on their movements, their marital options, their professional opportunities, and more. The Koran even rules that a son's inheritance should be twice the size of that of a daughter: "Allah (thus) directs you as regards your children's (inheritance): to the male, a portion equal to that of two females." (4:11).

In March 2007, a 19-year-old Saudi woman received a sentence of 90 lashes. Her crime? A man threatened to tell her father that they were having an affair unless she met him alone. When she did, she was kidnapped and repeatedly raped, after which her brother beat her because the rapes brought shame to the family. Rather than giving her justice, a Saudi court sentenced her to be lashed ninety times because she had met a man alone who was not related to her.

This was far from an isolated case. "In 2004, a sixteen-year-old girl, Atefeh Rajabi, was hanged in a public square in Iran. Her crime? Rajabi was charged with adultery—which probably means she was raped. Her rapist was not executed. Rajabi told the mullah-judge, Haji Rezaii, the he ought to punish men who rape, not their victims." The judge both sentenced and personally hanged Rajabi because, in addition to her crime, he said that she had "a sharp tongue." . . .

Several high-profile cases in Nigeria recently have also re-volved around rape accusations being transformed by Islamic authorities into charges of fornication. A seventeen-year-old Nigerian girl named Bariya Ibrahim Magazu, for instance, was sentenced to one hundred lashes for fornication after she was discovered to be pregnant. She accused several men of possi-bly being the father; when they all denied having had relations with her, she received an additional eighty lashes for false wit-ness. Islamic law restricts the validity of a woman's testimony, particularly in cases involving sexual immorality. And Islamic legal theorists have limited it even farther, in the words of one Muslim legal manual, to "cases involving property, or transac-tions dealing with property, such as sales." In other judicial ar-eas only men can testify. It is virtually impossible, therefore, to prove rape in lands that follow these *Sharia* [Islamic law] pro-visions. If the required male witnesses can't be found to exon-erate her (four men who testify to seeing the actual crime, ac-cording to the Koran), the victim's charge of rape can become an admission of adultery. That accounts for the grim fact that as many as seventy-five percent of the women in prison in Pa-kistan are, in fact, behind bars for the crime of having been raped.

Oppressive Attitudes Are Moving to the West

It is important to realize that such attitudes and behaviors which characterize Islamic gender apartheid have penetrated the West. There has been numerous reports of Muslim men raping women in Scandinavia and Australia. Their horrendous actions have been justified by imams. In September 2006, Australia's most senior Muslim cleric Sheikh Taj el-Din al-Hilali, in a clear reference to the notorious Sydney gang rap-ists, said in the sermon: "It is she who takes off her clothes, shortens them, flirts, puts on make-up and powder and takes to the streets, God protect us, dallying. If I came across a rape crime—kidnap and violation of honor—I would discipline the man and order that the woman be arrested and jailed for life. If she had not left the meat uncovered, the cat wouldn't have snatched it."

What must be understood is this: Any independent action taken by an Arab or Muslim girl or woman is perceived as intrinsically "sexual," "immoral," and "dishonorable." If she wants to attend college, refuses to marry a first cousin, chooses a love match, tries to elope, leaves her religion, converts to another religion—she runs the risk of being murdered in a highly eroticized way by woman-hating male mobs.

"The Koran is addressed to all Muslims, and for the most part it does not differentiate between male and female. Man and woman, it says, 'were created of a single soul,' and are moral equals in the sight of God."

Islam Does Not Oppress Women

Ruqaiyyah Waris Maqsood

Ruqaiyyah Waris Maqsood is a British Muslim author who served as the head of religious studies at William Gee High School in Hull, England. In the viewpoint that follows, Maqsood argues Islam treats women and men differently but as moral equals in the eyes of God. In Maqsood's view, women may not share all the same freedoms as women in Western societies, but this does not mean their rights are trampled or ignored under Islam. She maintains some Muslim nations have unusual laws that restrict women in various ways, but these laws are not dictated by scripture.

As you read, consider the following questions:

1. According to Maqsood, why does the Koran endorse polygamy?

Ruqaiyyah Waris Maqsood, "Islam, Culture and Women," *Islam For Today*. Reproduced by permission. www.islamfortoday.com.

2. As the author explains, when is divorce acceptable to Muslims and what steps should be taken first?

3. When is physical punishment of women condoned under Islam, as Maqsood reports?

How can anyone justify Islam's treatment of women, when it imprisons Afghans under blue shuttlecock burqas [a woman's garment that covers her, head to foot] and makes Pakistani girls marry strangers against their will?

How can you respect a religion that forces women into polygamous marriages, mutilates their genitals, forbids them to drive cars and subjects them to the humiliation of "instant" divorce? In fact, none of these practices are Islamic at all.

Anyone wishing to understand Islam must first separate the religion from the cultural norms and style of a society. Female genital mutilation is still practised in certain pockets of Africa and Egypt, but viewed as an inconceivable horror by the vast majority of Muslims. Forced marriages may still take place in certain Indian, Pakistani and Bangladeshi communities, but would be anathema to Muslim women from other backgrounds.

Indeed, Islam insists on the free consent of both bride and groom, so such marriages could even be deemed illegal under religious law.

A woman forbidden from driving a car in Riyadh [Saudi Arabia] will cheerfully take the wheel when abroad, confident that her country's bizarre law has nothing to do with Islam. Afghan women educated before the Taliban rule know that banning girls from school is forbidden in Islam, which encourages all Muslims to seek knowledge from cradle to grave, from every source possible.

The Koran Treats Both Sexes Fairly

The Koran is addressed to all Muslims, and for the most part it does not differentiate between male and female. Man and woman, it says, "were created of a single soul," and are moral

117

equals in the sight of God. Women have the right to divorce, to inherit property, to conduct business and to have access to knowledge.

Since women are under all the same obligations and rules of conduct as the men, differences emerge most strongly when it comes to pregnancy, child-bearing and rearing, menstruation and, to a certain extent, clothing.

Some of the commands are alien to Western tradition. Requirements of ritual purity may seem to restrict a woman's access to religious life, but are viewed as concessions. During menstruation or postpartum bleeding, she may not pray the ritual salah or touch the Koran and she does not have to fast; nor does she need to fast while pregnant or nursing.

The veiling of Muslim women is a more complex issue. Certainly, the Koran requires them to behave and dress modestly—but these strictures apply equally to men. Only one verse refers to the veiling of women, stating that the Prophet's [Muhammad's] wives should be behind a hijab when his male guests converse with them.

Some modernists, however, claim that this does not apply to women in general, and that the language used does not carry the textual stipulation that makes a verse obligatory. In practice, most modern Muslim women appreciate attractive and graceful clothes, but avoid dressing provocatively.

Islam Holds a Different Definition of Marriage

What about polygamy, which the Koran endorses up to the limit of four wives per man? The Prophet, of course, lived at a time when continual warfare produced large numbers of widows, who were left with little or no provision for themselves and their children.

In these circumstances, polygamy was encouraged as an act of charity. Needless to say, the widows were not necessarily

Are Women in the Muslim World Socialized To Expect Second-Class Status?

It is hardly unusual for women in predominantly Muslim countries in the Middle East and North Africa to have achieved higher education levels. The education "gender gap" ranged from zero in Iran, indicating no difference, to women needing to increase their levels 73% in Pakistan to equal that of men. . . .

In that light, it should be no surprise that most women in the Muslim world are well aware that they have the same capabilities and deserve the same fundamental rights as men. Majorities of females in each of the eight countries surveyed [Egypt, Iran, Jordan, Lebanon, Morocco, Pakistan, Saudi Arabia, and Turkey] said they believe women are able to make their own voting decisions, to work at any job for which they are qualified, and even to serve in the highest levels of government.

Dalia Mogahed,
"Perspectives of Women in the Muslim World,"
Gallup Poll Special Report: Muslim World, 2006.

sexy young women, but usually mothers of up to six children, who came as part of the deal.

Polygamy is no longer common, for various good reasons. The Koran states that wives need to be treated fairly and equally—a difficult requirement even for a rich man. Moreover, if a husband wishes to take a second wife, he should not do so if the marriage will be to the detriment of the first.

Sexual intimacy outside marriage is forbidden in Islam, including sex before marriage, adultery or homosexual relationships. However, within marriage, sexual intimacy should be raised from the animal level to sadaqah (a form of worship) so that each considers the happiness and satisfaction of the other, rather than mere self-gratification.

Contrary to Christianity, Islam does not regard marriages as "made in heaven" or "till death do us part". They are contracts, with conditions. If either side breaks the conditions, divorce is not only allowed, but usually expected. Nevertheless, a hadith [collection of the Prophet Muhammad's statements and actions coupled with the statements and actions of his companions] makes it clear that: "Of all the things God has allowed, divorce is the most disliked."

A Muslim has a genuine reason for divorce only if a spouse's behaviour goes against the sunnah [the established practices of earlier people, especially Arabs, and previous prophets] of Islam—in other words, if he or she has become cruel, vindictive, abusive, unfaithful, neglectful, selfish, sexually abusive, tyrannical, perverted—and so on.

In good Islamic practice, before divorce can be contemplated, all possible efforts should be made to solve a couple's problems. After an intention to divorce is announced, there is a three-month period during which more attempts are made at reconciliation.

If, by the end of each month, the couple have resumed sexual intimacy, the divorce should not proceed. The three-month rule ensures that a woman cannot remarry until three menstrual cycles have passed—so, if she happens to be pregnant, the child will be supported and paternity will not be in dispute.

How Islam Treats Men and Women Differently

When Muslims die, strict laws govern the shares of property and money they may leave to others; daughters usually inherit less than sons, but this is because the men in a family are supposed to provide for the entire household.

Any money or property owned by women is theirs to keep, and they are not obliged to share it. Similarly, in marriage, a woman's salary is hers and cannot be appropriated by her husband unless she consents.

A good Muslim woman, for her part, should always be trustworthy and kind. She should strive to be cheerful and encouraging towards her husband and family, and keep their home free from anything harmful (haram covers all aspects of harm, including bad behaviour, abuse and forbidden foods).

Regardless of her skills or intelligence, she is expected to accept her man as the head of her household—she must, therefore, take care to marry a man she can respect, and whose wishes she can carry out with a clear conscience. However, when a man expects his wife to do anything contrary to the will of God—in other words, any nasty, selfish, dishonest or cruel action—she has the right to refuse him.

Her husband is not her master; a Muslim woman has only one Master, and that is God. If her husband does not represent God's will in the home, the marriage contract is broken.

What should one make of the verse in the Koran that allows a man to punish his wife physically? There are important provisos: he may do so only if her ill-will is wrecking the marriage—but then only after he has exhausted all attempts at verbal communication and tried sleeping in a separate bed.

However, the Prophet never hit a woman, child or old person, and was emphatic that those who did could hardly regard themselves as the best of Muslims. Moreover, he also stated that a man should never hit "one of God's handmaidens." Nor, it must be said, should wives beat their husbands or become inveterate nags.

Moral Equals Under Islam

Finally, there is the issue of giving witness. Although the Koran says nothing explicit, other Islamic sources suggest that a woman's testimony in court is worth only half of that of a man. This ruling, however, should be applied only in circumstances where a woman is uneducated and has led a very restricted life: a woman equally qualified to a man will carry the same weight as a witness.

So, does Islam oppress women?

While the spirit of Islam is clearly patriarchal, it regards men and women as moral equals. Moreover, although a man is technically the head of the household, Islam encourages matriarchy in the home.

Women may not be equal in the manner defined by Western feminists, but their core differences from men are acknowledged, and they have rights of their own that do not apply to men.

| "Honor killing is a manifestation of global phenomenon in general and Muslim nations in particular."

Islam Condones Honor Killings

Syed Kamran Mirza

In the following viewpoint, Syed Kamran Mirza argues honor killings—the murder of female family members who are thought to have brought shame upon a family name—is condoned by the teachings of Islam. Mirza explains Islam supports such killings because of the religion's vehement condemnation of adultery and wanton fornication, two acts that incur shame to families. Mirza is the author of the book Four Articles on Roots of Terror in Islam. *He has also contributed opinion pieces to www.faith-freedom.org, the Web site of Faith Freedom International, which views Islam as an oppressive ideology.*

As you read, consider the following questions:

1. What acts by women in an Islamic society can bring shame upon a family's honor, according to Mirza?

2. What is the concept of *zina* in an Islamic society, and how does it factor into the author's argument?

Syed Kamran Mirza, "'Honor Killing' Is Absolutely Islamic," FaithFreedom.org, January 15, 2008. Reproduced by permission. www.news.faithfreedom.org.

3. According to the author, why does Islam consider a woman an "object of great shame?"

Honor killings, which occur with shocking regularity in certain parts of the Middle East and South Asia, target women whose actions—actual or suspected—violate the honor of their family, an honor which is thought to depend on the sexual purity of its female members. Victims are always killed/slaughtered mercilessly by her own family members. Honor killing is a manifestation of global phenomenon in general and Muslim nations in particular. Since this terrible inhumane practice exists only among the Muslims of the world—very often civilized people do blame Islam as the precursor of this dreadful act. Most others do not agree with this notion at all; and they try to put the blame on the tribal/cultural practice, and do not consider Islam is anyway responsible for it. In this [viewpoint] I shall analyze the real issues, cause and origin, and pattern of this heinous act amongst the Muslims of the world to postulate if there is any link, or incitements that originates from the very core of Islam.

What Is Honor Killing?

Honor killing is the bone chilling horrific cruelty committed by the family members—father, mother, brothers, brother-in-laws, even in some cases own sisters also. In this terrible episode the victim is always the daughter/sister or other blood related young women who gets killed. Perpetrators are always the family members stated above. Family honor is one of the core values of Arab society. Anything from speaking with an unrelated man, to rumored pre-marital loss of virginity, to an extramarital affair, [refusing] forced marriages, [marrying] according to their will; or even women and girls who have been raped—can stain or destroy the family honor. Therefore, family members (parents, brothers, or sisters) kill the victim in order to remove the stain or maintain, and protect the honor of the family. Killers are given light sentences, sometimes with little or no jail time at all. The killers mainly defend their act of murder by referring to the Koran and Islam. Family guardian will say that they are merely following the directives set down in their Islamic ethical beliefs.

These barbaric killings occur only to save the honor of the family, and not for any animosity or for wealth or gold. In 100% of cases—the killers have no animosity, rather they love the girl as their own daughter or sister, but they kill the girl anyway upon their ethical compulsion to save their family honor, or to erase family stigmas. The victims cry, beg for their life but the family members become merciless (out of their ethical prejudices and also religious burden of fear) and kill the victim. After killing family members usually mourn and cry for the victim (usually loving daughter or sister) but feel solace that they have done the right thing to save their family honor.

And this kind of cruel killings to save family honor [has] happened, [is] still happening and will [continue] to happen—only to a Muslim family. Honor killings happen only to some designated Muslim nations such as Saudi Arabia, Jordan, Syria, Yemen, Lebanon, Egypt, Sudan, the Gaza strip and the West Bank (Palestine), Jordan, Pakistan, Indonesia, Malaysia, Nigeria, Somalia, Turkey, Iran and some other south and central Asian countries. Bangladesh—though a Muslim majority country—[has never had a] regular pattern of honor killings . . . as of today. . . .

Honor Killing Is a Cultural/Tribal Phenomenon

Most Muslim apologists and also some gullible Westerners want to argue that the so called "honor of killing" is not Islamic [but rather] it's a tribal/cultural vice. This statement is utterly untrue and only a wishful cover up. It's true that in pre-Islamic Arab culture this heinous honor killing of women did exist; likewise, many other uncivilized practices like ston-

Domestic Violence in Egypt

In the field of gender based violence, CWELA [the Egyptian Association of Legal Aid for Women] started compiling and analyzing press coverage of 20 daily newspapers and weekly magazines that dealt with domestic violence in Egypt during the period mid 2002 till mid 2003. CEWLA's report showed the geographical distribution of the different incidences of domestic violence among the different governorates in Egypt. The report also showed that the perpetrators of violence were males in 75% of the cases and women represented 25%. The perpetrators were the husbands (52%), the fathers (10%), the brothers (10%), the mothers (4%) the rest were the sons, relatives of the husband or of the wife, the step-father or the step-mother. The types of violence were murder (76%), attempt to murder (5%), battering (18%), kidnapping (2.5%) and the rest were different types such as burning property, forcing women to sign cheques and become guarantors of men, accusation of insanity ..., etc. The report indicated that causes of violence were honour crimes (42%), leaving the house without the husband's approval (7.5%), wives asking for divorce (3%) ..., etc.

Fatma Khafagy,
"Honour Killing in Egypt,"
Association of Legal Aid for Women,
May 2005. www.un.org/womenwatch/daw.

ing, flogging, beheading, slavery, etc., also existed in the pre-Islamic Arab society. But Islam did incorporate entirely most of these inhumane/uncivilized practices of pagan society, [and] they now call them Allah's laws. . . .

Honor killing does happen only amongst the Muslims and these honor killings get support and encouragement from the ethical teachings of ... Islam. ... It has been reported that in Pakistan and in Jordan several hundreds of "honor killings" do happen every year. Perhaps, it will be more plausible to name this so called 'honor' as the "Islamic honor", which Muslims stupendously try to save by killing their loved one!. ...

Adultery in Islam

The Arabic word 'Zina' means all extramarital sexual intercourse between a man and a woman. According to Islam 'Zina' constituted social suicide—an entire society commits suicide over time if it allows fornication and adultery to go unpunished in the Islamic style. As per Islamic justice—unmarried fornicators receive a hundred stripes [lashes], but married adulterers must die by stoning, as described in the *sahih hadiths*.

The Saudi Ambassador to London [England], Ghazi al-Qusaibi, says that stoning may seem irrational to the Western mind, but it is "at the core of the Islamic faith." An intellectual, the Saudi ambassador to London asserted that stoning adulterers to death is a legitimate punishment for society. He also says that Westerners should respect Muslim culture on this matter.

Sheikh Ahmad Kutty, a senior lecturer and Islamic scholar at the Islamic Institute of Toronto, Ontario, Canada, states, "Adultery in Islam is one of the most heinous and deadliest of sins. Its enormity can be gauged from the fact that it has often been conjoined in the Qur'an with the gravest of all sins: shirk or associating partners with Allah."

Hani Ramadan head of the Islamic Center in Geneva [Switzerland] (Hani Ramadan is the elder brother of famed Swiss Muslim intellectual Tarek Ramadan, who are both the grandsons of Hassan Al-Banna, the founder of Egypt's outlawed Muslim Brotherhood.) stated, "Islam has taken a firm

and decisive stance against Zina (fornication or adultery). Allah, the Almighty, commands in explicit and unequivocal
words: 'And come not near unto adultery. Lo! it is an abomi-
nation and an evil way.' (Al-Isra: 32)." . . .

Women in Muslim Society

According to Islamic tradition the woman is an object owned
by the man who assumes responsibility for her behavior and
her life. The social and religious traditions lead to the isolation of the woman in her home. She is required to cover her
entire body in order to maintain the honor of the man. In
[the] Qur'an, prophetic tradition and law, one finds a very
strong presumption of women's chastity along with numerous
safeguards to prevent any imputation of un-chastity. A Muslim feminist/sexual ethics must help create the conditions for
the Qur'anic and traditional values of modesty and chastity to
be lived by Muslim women and men in ways that are faith-
fully chosen and equitably maintained.

A woman who is either raped or commits adultery becomes the source of shame to her family. People will not
marry her because she has been spoiled; she and her family
become the object of gossip of everyone in the society; hence
the entire family can lose prestige. No one would give a daughter to the brothers of that girl in marriage and no one would
marry her sisters. The family and even the extended family are
maligned and become outcasts. This can only stop if the family cleanses that stain with blood. The woman thus defiled
must be killed even if she is a victim of rape.

Islam is dreadfully anti-women. This statement can be
proven with 100% guarantee by the well-known and established fact that women folks in every Muslim country in general, and in every Islamic paradise (country where Islamic
Shariaat [the code of law derived from the Koran and from
the teachings and example of Mohammed] is enforced) in
particular, are severely subjugated, oppressed, and considered

less than second class citizen. Women in Islam are considered half human and in the Quran women have half the rights of men, sister has half the rights of brother, and women are considered deficient in intelligence.

Practically and literally, Islam considers women as the sources of great shame. Prophet Muhammed said women are *awrah* which can be translated as object of shame. What is awrah? *The Encyclopedia of Islam* defines 'awrah' as pudendum, which is the external genitals, especially of the female. The word Pudendum derives from the Latin pudor which means sense of shame and modesty. Therefore, awrah signify an object of shame that needs to be covered. . . .

Muslims who are stunningly devout and laden with Islamic superstitious beliefs do commit crime of honor killing to fulfill their obligation of preserving Islamic ethics, and women chastity. The more a country gets fanatically religious the more frequent are honor killings (Pakistan is a perfect example). Islam has incorporated many pre-Islamic practices of Arab pagans (stoning deaths, flogging the fornicators, slavery, war booty, beheading the criminal, cutting hands and [feet off] thieves, many rituals of animal sacrifice, annual pilgrimage to Mecca, etc.) and readily called them Islamic or Allah's laws. Honor killing is one such pre-Islamic practice of Arab pagans which has been practicing by some devout Muslim families of many good Islamic nations of the world.

> *"Given that honor killings are a global phenomenon and not isolated to Muslims, how do critics justify their anger toward only one group?"*

Islam Does Not Condone Honor Killings

Robert Wagner

Robert Wagner is a journalist and the operator of the 13 Martyrs blog, which serves as a discussion platform focusing on civil liberty issues and world events. In the following viewpoint, Wagner argues Islam is unfairly blamed for promoting honor killings. Wagner contends honor killings occur in many nations—both Muslim and non-Muslim—and have nothing to do with religion. He believes until honor killings are viewed as having no connection to Islam, Muslim communities will bear unjust backlash from societies already torn by perceived religious and ethnic differences.

As you read, consider the following questions:

1. According to Wagner, why should honor killing not be considered a gender issue?

2. What evidence does Wagner give to support his argument that Islam is not responsible for honor killings?

Robert Wagner, "The Myth of Muslim Honor Killings," 13 Martyrs, January 7, 2008. Reproduced by permission. http://13martyrs.blogspot.com.

3. According to Wagner, why should those angry about honor killing focus their anger on governments as opposed to religious groups?

The tragic deaths of Aqsa Parvez and Amina and Sarah Said have raised the specter of honor killings within the Muslim communities in Ontario, Canada, and in Texas [respectively]. The leading newspapers in Toronto, Dallas and Fort Worth have been circumspect in their coverage, but it hasn't stemmed the scorn heaped on Muslims from readers and television viewers who see these murders through the prism of religion and 9/11 [2001 terrorist attacks].

To many, these three very Westernized teenage girls were killed because their fathers believed they brought shame on the families.

The Parvez and Said families have been unequivocal in their statements to the media that the slayings were not honor killings and had nothing to do with religion. Islam Said, brother of Amina, 18, and Sarah, 17, clearly has no sympathy for his father, Yaser, accused of killing his daughters. He told local media that, "I just hope he turns himself in because, you know, he messed up the whole family."

These assertions have been dismissed as either denial or just plain lying to protect the perpetrators of these crimes. Curiously, the harshest critics of Islam know that the Qur'an and Sharia [Islamic law] make no mention of honor killings and condemn murder.

Honor Killing Occurs in All Faiths

It's pointless to quote the Qur'an's condemnation of murder or to point out the numerous passages in the Bible that condone killing women who dishonor men or God. Nor will I provide a history lesson on the patriarchal societies, Muslim and non-Muslim, that encourage these kinds of crimes. Rather, I will focus on the evidence at hand that clearly demonstrates the insidious nature of honor killings that crosses religious, cultural and gender boundaries.

It's impossible to simplify the complex nature of honor killings by labeling it a religious or cultural disease. No one can make a case that honor killing is a religious issue because there is no justification for it in the Qur'an or Sharia and it occurs in all religions.

If honor killings were strictly a Muslim issue, how can it be explained that such murders are virtually unheard of in Indonesia, the most populous Muslim country, and in Saudi Arabia, the land of the two holy mosques and the most conservative Muslim country? In fact, the evidence is overwhelming that not only are Muslims responsible for only a portion of honor killings but the killings are committed on a global scale that includes Hindus, Sikhs, Christians and people of no faith.

Non-Muslim Honor Killing

The latest example of a non-Muslim honor killing occurred [December] 29 [2007] in Oak Forest, Illinois, when Subhash Chander, an Indian, set a fire that killed his pregnant daughter, his son-in-law and his 3-year-old grandson because he disapproved of his daughter's marriage. Chander was upset with his daughter and her husband because they had married without his consent and that Kumar was from a lower caste in India than Rani's family.

Yet these murders received little attention outside the Chicago area and virtually none from critics attacking Muslims for perceived honor killings.

These critics ignore the universal nature of honor killings. In September 2006, the BBC conducted a poll that found that honor killings crossed all religions. The poll of 500 Hindus, Sikhs, Christians and Muslims found that one in 10 believed that honor killings are justified.

Focusing on Honor Killings Detracts from the Larger Issue of Universal Patriarchal Violence

To deny or ignore the existence of a culture of struggle for gender equality in ... non-Western societies is a political decision emanating from patriarchal politics, in the sense that to do so denies the universality of the oppression of women and the struggle against it. It is racist in so far as it denies to non-Western, non-white women the means to understand the conditions surrounding their subordination and ignores their determination to resist. . . .

The culture of patriarchal violence is . . . universal. To divide cultures into violent and violence-free is itself a patriarchal myth. And we have what amounts to an ethnocentric or racist myth when this divide is drawn along the lines of West and East. Moreover, while the existence of patriarchy as a culture cannot be denied, a culturally reductionist approach alone does not take us a long way in the struggle against male violence.

Shahrzad Mojab,
"Thoughts on the Struggle against 'Honor Killing,'"
International Journal of Kurdish Studies, *January 2002.*

It's also impossible to argue that it's a geographical or cultural phenomenon because these murders transcend all cultures. And it's not even a gender issue since many women are complicit in the planning and execution of the murders and that many victims are men. Amnesty International says that "females in the family—mothers, mothers-in-law, sisters, and cousins—frequently support the attacks. It's a community mentality."

Islam Online reported in January 2007 that between 2000 and 2006 about 4,000 Pakistanis were slain in honor killings. An estimated 2,774 of the victims were women and 1,226 were men.

Also consider that within one five-year period, more than 1,000 women were kidnapped and murdered in Guatemala. Their bodies were usually mutilated and in some cases "death to bitches" was written on them. And in Juarez, Mexico, hundreds of women were kidnapped, murdered and buried. The killers remain free.

In 2006 a Catholic Italian man shot his sister to death for having a child out of wedlock. Up until 1991, men in Brazil could be absolved of killing their wives over honor. In Yemen, a Jewish father killed his daughter after a rabbi complained that she had a child from an affair. And a Christian father beat his daughter to death in 2005 in Palestine because she wanted to marry a Muslim. [In 2007] in Bashika, Mosul, a 17-year-old woman, a member of the Yezidi religion was stoned to death for having an Arab Muslim boyfriend.

UNICEF [the United Nations Children's Fund] reports that more than 5,000 non-Muslim women are killed in so-called dowry deaths each year in India because their in-laws consider their dowries inadequate.

Human Rights Watch considers dowry deaths the same as honor killings because of similar dynamics in which the victims are killed by male members of the family and because the crimes are excused or understood by the community.

Secular Governments Approve of Honor Killings

Further evidence that Islam either as a religion or a culture is not responsible for many of these murders is that some governments approve of honor killings. Jordan and Syria, for example, are governments made up of secular laws. Jordan, in particular, has a mishmash of codes that include Islamic, tribal, European and some international laws. The Qur'an, unlike in Saudi Arabia, does not serve as the constitution of these two countries. And neither use Sharia. Rather, legislation exists that provides minimal or no punishment to murders committed in the name of family honor.

As a result, an estimated 200 to 300 honor killings are committed in Syria each year. About 25 honor slayings are committed annually in Jordan and about 60 a year in Turkey, another Muslim country that is governed by secular laws. If anger is to be directed to those responsible for encouraging honor killings, it should be the governments that allow legislation to be passed that protects the killers.

Islam Condemns Honor Killings

Do Muslims as a rule condone honor killings? Of course not. Syria's grand mufti [interpreter of Islamic law], cleric Ahmad Hassoun, has condemned the crime as un-Islamic. Forty Pakistani religious scholars issued a joint fatwa [a legal pronouncement] in 2006 against honor killings, branding the practice as contrary to the teachings of Prophet Muhammad. And [in 2007] Lebanon's Grand Ayatollah Mohammed Hussein Fadlallah issued a fatwa banning honor killings, characterizing the practice as a "repulsive act."

In 2000, members of the Jordanian royal family led 4,000 demonstrators in protest against Jordanian laws that allow men who kill in the name of honor to go free. And Queen Rania has been a tireless critic of Jordanian laws protecting honor killers and has waged a campaign to repeal those laws.

Given that honor killings are a global phenomenon and not isolated to Muslims, how do critics justify their anger toward only one group? They can't, but it won't stop them from letting the facts get in the way of their agenda.

We live in a society that labels and demonizes certain groups to justify their hatred. Americans, in particular, have a nasty habit throughout history of targeting specific groups—

from the American Indian to Japanese-Americans to communists and now Muslims—to justify their fear and anger. There is no logic to it. It makes no sense. But it makes people feel as if they are helping their country by attacking perceived enemies.

Periodical Bibliography

The following articles have been selected to supplement the diverse views presented in this chapter.

Lorraine Adams	"Beyond the Burka," *New York Times Book Review*, January 6, 2008.
Lorraine Ali	"Only One Side of the Story," *Newsweek*, February 26, 2007.
Nadia Ali	"The Mainstream Modest Muslim Woman," *Islaamic Magazine (I-MAG)*, Summer 2007.
Dave Belden	"Ayaan Hirsi Ali: An Islamic Feminist Leaves Islam," *Tikkun*, July/August 2007.
Lisa Beyer	"The Women of Islam," *Time*, December 3, 2001.
Toni Briegel and Jaye Zivkovic	"Financial Empowerment of Women in the United Arab Emirates," *Journal of Middle East Women's Studies*, Spring 2008.
Moira Dustin and Anne Phillips	"Whose Agenda Is It?: Abuses of Women and Abuses of 'Culture' in Britain," *Ethnicities*, September 2008.
Economist	"Our Women Must Be Protected," April 26, 2008.
Fatemeh Fakhraie	"Hate the Veil: A New Look at an Old Practice," *Bitch Magazine: Feminist Response to Pop Culture*, Fall 2008.
Ziauddin Sardar	"Forced Marriages Disgrace Islam," *New Statesman*, March 31, 2008.
Helena Smith	"Women on the Streets," *New Statesman*, May 21, 2007.
Irfan Yusuf	"Something Rotten in Islam," *Eureka Street*, October 24, 2008.

OPPOSING
VIEWPOINTS®
SERIES

CHAPTER 4

What Is the Future of Islam?

Chapter Preface

Various media pundits have described Islam as the fastest growing religion in the world. Such a claim is meant to suggest Muslims will eventually—through birthrate and conversion—dominate global societies, forever changing the character of the Western world. Conservative columnist Mark Steyn attests the number of adherents is, to him, a frightening aspect of Islam's ascendancy, but he is also keenly aware of another demographic feature that could be more troubling to those who feel the West is being eclipsed. In his book *America Alone: The End of the World As We Know It*, Steyn asserts the vast majority of the Muslim world is under 30 years of age. In comparison, Steyn notes European nations are suffering low birth rates and that most Westernized nations are coping with larger graying populations. The result of this demographic fact is obvious to Steyn: "A people who won't multiply can't go forth or go anywhere. Those who do will shape the age we live in."

As Steyn admits, the sheer number of young Muslims alone does not guarantee some form of global supremacy. In his view, youth must be wedded to a strong will for Islam to effect large social change. But, more worrisome to Steyn, is the West seems particularly inert in the face of such a predicament. He maintains the focus of Western nations is on increasing welfare programs for their aging populations, not on fending off an Islamic tidal wave. In addition, Steyn believes in the United States the welfare state is eroding self-reliance and other individualistic virtues that might spur Americans to take action. Furthermore, he claims this enervation is coupled with a dangerous belief in cultural relativism that has taught Americans and other Westerners to overvalue foreign cultures and passively accept their growing global impact. The consequence, Steyn believes, will be felt very soon. He writes, "In a few years, as millions of Muslim teenagers are entering their voting booths, some European countries will not be living formally under sharia [Islamic law], but . . . they will have reached an accommodation with their radicalized Islamic compatriots, who like many intolerant types are expert at exploiting the 'tolerance' of pluralist societies."

Whether Steyn's view of the future of Islam will come to pass is as yet unknown. Many Islamic thinkers argue it is Muslim territories who are currently on the defensive. Anas Altikriti, a spokesperson for the Muslim Association of Britain, states, "Muslims do not want to conquer the world—on the contrary, it is their lands that are being conquered bit by bit at the hands of Western forces." In the following chapter, several other commentators offer their predictions of what the future will hold for Islam and Muslims.

| "Darwinists respect only strength and they yield only to the type of pressures that they can feel with their five senses."

Muslims Must Oppose Western Consumerist Culture

Abdel-Wahab Elmessiri

In the following viewpoint, Abdel-Wahab Elmessiri claims Western civilization is guided by a rapacious capitalist philosophy, one that sees the Muslim world as merely a land of resources that can be used to further consumerism. Elmessiri argues the resistance of Islamic values to this form of Darwinian modernism—in which only the strongest nations will ultimately survive—is thwarting the West's goals and earning its wrath. While Elmessiri believes the West and the East have many shared interests, he nonetheless asserts Muslim resistance is necessary because the West's Darwinian ideology can be countered only by a show of force. Elmessiri was an Egyptian professor of English and the author of The Encyclopedia of the Jews, Judaism, and Zionism: A New Explanatory Paradigm. *He died in 2008.*

Abdel-Wahab Elmessiri, "Why the West Attacks Us," *Al-Ahram Weekly*, September 13–19, 2007. Reproduced by permission. http://weekly.ahram.org.eg.

141

As you read, consider the following questions:

1. What does Elmessiri see as the similarities between Christian and Islamic creeds?

2. The author states the West is not hostile to Islam but is hostile to what?

3. Why does Elmessiri not believe there is a clash of civilizations between the West and the East?

Our relationship with the West began with Alexander the Great, the founder of the colonialist Ptolemaic Dynasty that ruled Egypt and the Levant for several hundred years. In that distant past there existed a form of parity; a certain give and take, an alternation of victory and defeat between the two sides. Even to today, however, it is possible to point to factors that can as easily form the basis of mutual understanding and cooperation between Islam and the West as they can trigger conflict. For example, we share with some Western nations the border of the Mediterranean, whose importance for trade and maritime wealth should compel neighbours on either side towards closer cooperation, especially in this age of the global village.

Yet that very proximity has also been the source of intense friction because of the lure of land and resources on the other side. In its height, Islamic civilisation expanded geographically at the expense of the West as defined by the ambit of Christian civilisation, and the reverse was also true: the expansion of the West took place at the expense of the Islamic world, and tensions reached a zenith when Western powers moved to partition that world amongst themselves. Conversely, the further removed societies and civilisations are from one another geographically, the lower the potential for conflict between them. At least before the rise of Western colonialism, which staked out the entire world as its field of enterprise, there existed no tension between the West and Thailand, for example, simply because land and resources were so far out of reach.

Commonalities Between Islam and Christianity

There are many similarities between the Muslim and Christian creeds that, similarly, could motivate closer communication and understanding just as they could also exacerbate tensions. Islam and Christianity share the belief in a single transcendent universal deity who has sent mankind holy books to guide them. The moral and ethical systems contained in these books are similar in many respects and could, therefore, serve as a common ground between the two religions and a framework of moral authority to which peoples of both could appeal. History in Islam and Christianity has an ultimate aim, in which mankind figures centrally; in both the existence of man on earth is not futile or absurd. The stories of creation in Islam and Christianity are similar: God breathed His spirit into matter He created from the void, thereby imparting in man certain qualities (a body and a soul, the capacity for good and evil, and other such dualities) that distinguish him from other creatures.

These very commonalties between the two creeds can also constitute a source of tension between their respective adherents. The West is reluctant to classify Islam as an autonomous creed with its own vision of the universe. In spite of commonalties—or rather because of them—it regards Islam's rejection of incarnation, of a clerical interface between worshippers and God, and of elaborate rites and rituals and the mystical concepts these engender as deviations from Christianity and heresies. (The West does not adopt this approach towards such Eastern religions such as Shinto and Buddhism; because they are so far removed from Christianity in their view of the universe and doctrines, the West regards them as distinct and authentic creeds in their own right.) But Islam behaves similarly: it regards the New Testament as a holy

Reacting Against Secularism and Modernism

Ultimately, the struggle of the fundamentalists is against two enemies, secularism and modernism. The war against secularism is conscious and explicit, and there is by now a whole literature denouncing secularism as an evil neo-pagan force in the modern world and attributing it variously to the Jews, the West, and the United States. The war against modernity is for the most part neither conscious nor explicit, and is directed against the whole process of change that has taken place in the Islamic world in the past century or more and has transformed the political, economic, social, and even cultural structures of Muslim countries. Islamic fundamentalism has given an aim and a form to the otherwise aimless and formless resentment and anger of the Muslim masses at the forces that have devalued their traditional values and loyalties and, in the final analysis, robbed them of their beliefs, their aspirations, their dignity, and to an increasing extent even their livelihood.

Bernard Lewis, "The Roots of Muslim Rage,"
Policy, *Summer 2001–2002.*

book that has been tampered with and distorted by Christians themselves and it regards itself and its own revealed text as the only true religion.

The Green Peril

Another factor that works to create a gulf between the Islamic and Western worlds is that each defines its own identity with respect to the other. Generally such a phenomenon is normal, but when it is taken to the extreme it becomes pernicious, because of latent antagonism bred by the antithesis. Since the middle of the 19th century, the West sounded the alarm against the "yellow peril" (China) and then the "red peril" (Communism). Now that these bugbears have been put to rest, it has begun to speak of the "green peril" (Islam).

Temperatures have risen recently between the Western and Islamic worlds with the growing influx into Europe of immigrants from Islamic societies bordering Europe (notably Turks, Moroccans and Kurds). One would think that these immigrant communities could have formed a bridge of understanding between the two worlds. However, because of declining birth rates in Western societies (even in Catholic societies, which once had high rates) at a time when Muslims still adhere to their traditional epistemological and ethical systems, and because of increasing secularisation in the West, Westerners have also raised the spectre of the Muslim demographic threat.

A related phenomenon that tends to fuel animosity between the West and Islam today is "Eurocentrism", by which is meant the tendency to view others, and specifically Muslims and peoples of the Third World, through a purely European perspective and to pass judgement on those societies or peoples in terms of European cultural values. In this sense, therefore, the West's war against the Islamic world is a religious one. But religion, here, is not just doctrine and ritual, but a fundamental component of the Muslim's universal perspective and sociopolitical identity.

If most of the factors above could either serve to promote reconciliation and mutual understanding or ignite and fuel acrimony and antagonism, why has the latter tendency prevailed at this time? Why, in other words, has the relationship between the West and Islam become so openly hostile? Why has "terrorism" in the war on terrorism become synonymous with Islam?

The West's Rapacious Consumerism

Surely one of the foremost factors to have fanned the flames between the West and the Islamic world is the West's Darwinian modernism, which has translated itself into a voracious consumerism requiring an imperialist edifice with an unquenchable thirst for the world's energy resources to feed it. Most of the world's energy resources happen to be situated in the Islamic world. It is little wonder, therefore, that the modernist imperialist order fired by its rabid consumerism set its predatory sights on this part of the planet and swooped down so rapidly on Afghanistan and Iraq. It needed to get its clutches on the world's largest reserves of oil, in the Caspian Sea and in the Middle East, in order to protect its national security, as it defines it, and safeguard the flow of oil at reasonable prices and in sufficient quantifies to nourish exponentially growing consumer demand in the US and elsewhere in the West.

The West is not hostile to Islam, per se. It is hostile to a resistant Islam, an Islam that challenges the West's Darwinism and consumerism. A docile and obsequious Islam is something else; the West is perfectly willing to accept and work with this. Western antagonism towards Islam is not of an abstract metaphysical order; it has tangible historical roots. When this part of the world attempted to resist the onslaught of Western colonialism via the banner of Arab nationalism, the West allied itself with Islamist movements against Arab nationalism. It was only when Arab nationalism receded and Arab resistance raised an Islamic banner that the West began to lash out at Islam. Remember, [terrorist leader Osama] Bin Laden was originally trained by the US to fight Washington's war against the Soviets in Afghanistan.

Western Darwinian modernism is not only hostile towards resistant Islam, but also towards all movements that espouse humanitarian values. It, therefore, opposes left-wing Christian groups that defend the poor and environmentalist groups. But it nonetheless perceives Islam as the greatest potential threat. As such, the West does not perceive Muslims and Arabs as autonomous human societies with their own legitimate aspirations and goals, but rather as pliable matter that must be made to submit and be forced into an iron cage—the cage of ever spiralling production and consumption for the sole purpose of material comfort and worldly pleasure. For us merely to suggest other values and aspirations, such as attachment to the land, the defence of pride and dignity, the rejection of laws of competition as the ultimate arbiter, is to doom ourselves to being pegged, in Western eyes, as irrational creatures.

Resistance to the Capitalist Mode of Civilization

There has been much talk, recently, of the "clash of civilisations," by which is generally meant a clash between Islamic civilisation (or Oriental civilisations in general) and Western civilisation. I do not believe the concept holds water. History is replete with evidence of considerable positive and constructive interaction between the two. Even in the modern colonialist era, the Islamic world opened itself to many Western ideas, not to mention modern technology and goods. But while there is no "clash of civilisations," I would suggest that there exists a clash over the mode of civilisation.

Many in the Islamic world as well as in the West abhor the rapacious capitalism that accords the highest value to ever increasing production and consumer rates and that believes it the right of the militarily fittest to protect this economic order at home at the expense of others abroad; to send out armies to seize control over the energy and mineral resources that feed this order, to create and support proxy governments to assist it in its rapaciousness, to open their markets to its products and to kowtow to the global economic system. This insatiable consumerist capitalism is not identical with Western civilisation, but rather only one of many trends within that civilisation.

Many in the West have been deeply distressed at how this trend has succeeded in manoeuvring itself into power in the US and propelling the world to war and doing whatever it could to promote the interests of big business at the expense of the poor and disadvantaged and to the lasting detriment to the global environment. The millions who took to the streets in Europe and the US to protest American intervention in Iraq are indicative of growing opposition there to rampant capitalism. I believe that we in the Islamic world should ally ourselves with representatives of that trend in the interest of putting a stop to Washington's military rampage in the world.

Islam Must Continue To Resist

There is a very real possibility for dialogue and mutual under-standing. However, we must first take stock of the fact that the ruling elite in the West, with its Darwinian imperialist vision, is irrational. Rationalism presumes the existence of humani-tarian and moral criteria that stand on their own as absolutes above the fray of human selfishness and bias. So how are we supposed to talk in the absence of a set of moral humanitar-ian criteria that all are willing to respect and abide by? Clearly, dialogue alone is not sufficient. Nor are media campaigns, however forceful. We must sustain the resistance, for other-wise the Darwinian mentality will perceive our willingness to engage in dialogue as a sign of weakness and our media cam-paigns as a sign of laziness. Darwinists respect only strength and they yield only to the type of pressures that they can feel with their five senses, since it is impossible to appeal to their minds that are unable to apply rational humanitarian thought. Dialogue will only succeed when backed by strength and the power of resistance.

> "Peace and justice are comprehensive concepts with deep implications and we have to be people committed to peace and justice."

Muslims Must Promote Peace and Justice

Zaid Shakir

Zaid Shakir is an African American Muslim scholar and spiritual leader (imam) who teaches Islamic studies at the Zaytuna Institute in Berkeley, California. In the following viewpoint, an excerpt from his book Scattered Pictures: Reflections of an American Muslim, *Shakir explains how Islamic verse and the words of the Prophet Muhammad demand Muslims live by the principles of justice and peace. To Shakir, both concepts do not represent passive states but rather must be actively exhibited in personal relationships and extended to global affairs so all may benefit from them.*

As you read, consider the following questions:

1. How does Shakir view warfare under his definition of peace?

Zaid Shakir, *Scattered Pictures: Reflections of an American Muslim.* IslamiCity.com, 2005. Reproduced by permission of Zaytuna Institute.

2. On what single verse from the Qur'an does the classical theologian Ibn Taymiyya insist the responsibilities of Islamic governments should be based?

3. As Shakir implies, what is commutative justice?

W e are living in a world where there could obviously be more peace. As Muslims, we realize this fact more than most people, as the peace of many of our brothers and sisters in various parts of the globe has been tragically disrupted: Palestine, Chechnya, Afghanistan, Kashmir, and other locales. Similarly, we are living in a world where there could be more justice. We read almost daily of assassinations in various parts of the world where terrorist groups, military forces, or intelligence services, oftentimes in summary fashion, declare victims guilty and then proceed to execute them. Unfortunately, such unprincipled political behavior has become increasingly common in both the foreign and domestic policies of this country, causing untold damage to her image and credibility abroad.

These two issues, peace and justice, are joined in the slogans we hear from many activists, especially here in the United States, "No Justice, No Peace!"[1] This linkage is logical, as justice must be considered one of the indispensable prerequisites of any lasting peace. This article intends to briefly look at the ideas of peace and justice in Islam and explore their deeper significance in the life of a Muslim.

Peace

In the Arabic language, the word peace is derived from the radicals S-L-M. The scholars of language mention four closely related terms that can be derived from this origin: *Salam, Salamah, Silm,* and *Salm.* Raghib al-Isfahani says in his lexicon of Qur'anic terms, "As-Salm and as-Salamah mean freedom from any external or internal ruination."[2] Based on that, he mentions that true peace will only exist in Paradise, for only there will there be perpetuity with no end, complete satisfaction with no need, perfect honor with no humiliation, and perfect health with no disease. In this regard, God is known as As-Salam, because He alone is described as being totally free from any defects or flaws.[3] This understanding of true peace being a reality associated with a transformed world is also understood in both Jewish and Christian theology.[4]

At the level of interstate relations, if we ponder the above definition, we can consider peaceful relations between nations as a condition where violence, a state inevitably involving both internal and external ruination, is absent. In this sense, war can be viewed as an aberrational state. The aberrational nature of war is made clearer if we consider that murder, the ultimate consequence of war, is considered an innovation that destroyed the peace formerly existing among the human family. It is stated in a prophetic tradition, "No soul is killed unjustly, except that the elder son of Adam (Cain) shares in the stain of the crime. That is because he was the first to innovate murder [in the human family]."[5]

At the individual level, peace can be viewed as an absence of the ruinations of the heart. One free from such ruinations will succeed, God-willing, when he/she meets his/her Lord. Therefore, he/she will enter safely into the Abode of Peace (Dar as-Salam). God says in that regard, [On] the day no amount of wealth or children will be of any benefit. [The only one benefited] will be one who comes before God with a sound (salim) heart. [Quran 26:89]

If one reflects on these meanings, it should be clear that the wars that Muslims have been involved in throughout our long history do not nullify the validity of the statement, "Islam is the religion of peace," what is meant by that expression, and God knows best, is that Islam provides a path for the human being to enter Paradise (Dar as-Salam), and there he/she will know true peace.

Peace has meanings wider than those mentioned above. One of the loftier objectives of our religion is to introduce into the world an ethos that facilitates the spreading of peace at every level. Our personal relations with our fellow Muslims should begin with the implementation of the Prophetic order "Spread peace between you all."[6] This order is so pressing that the Beloved Prophet advised its indiscriminate implementation. He said at the end of a tradition in which he described one of the best forms of Islam, "Extend the greeting of peace, to those you know and those you know not."[7] This is a very weighty matter that calls for our deeper reflection. Its weightiness is illustrated by the fact that it is mentioned as being one of the things that completes our faith. The Prophet said in that regard, "You will not enter Paradise until you believe, and you will not believe until you love one another. Shall I indicate to you something that will surely lead to your mutual love? Spread the greeting and spirit of peace between yourselves."[8]

Our relations with our spouses should also be characterized by peace. God admonishes us concerning those relations, And peace is best. [Quran 4:128] Similarly, in our relations with other nations, God commands us, If they (the enemy) incline towards peace, then you should similarly incline, and place your trust in God. [Quran 8:61] As mentioned above, peace is the original state that prevailed in relations between individuals and societies. This opinion is based, among other narrations, on the saying of the Prophet that Jesus "will return the world to a state of peace" (Yurji' as-Salim) after his appearance at the end of time.[9]

Justice

Our lexicographers define justice, variously, as "to rule based on that contained in the Book of God and the tradition (Sunna) of His Messenger and refraining from ruling based on empty opinion." It is also defined as "extending inherent rights [to their possessors] equitably."[10] This latter definition emphasizes the importance of equity as an essential aspect of distributive justice.

Liberty and Justice: Two Pillars of Islamic Liberalism

Hurriya (liberty)—Human beings are created free and must remain free; freedom of thought, freedom of religion, and freedom of movement are essential to life as envisaged by our creator. Without freedom, life and religion have no meaning and no flavor. God, in his unlimited wisdom, intended human beings to be free; free to believe or disbelieve and free to practice or not practice. It is wrong and counterproductive to impose religion on people, and it is also against the will of God.

Adl (justice)—Equality before God must translate into equality on earth. Only God can be the judge of who is best among us. Justice must be upheld for everyone—man or woman, Muslim or non-Muslim, friend or foe, Arab or non-Arab. Justice means that every human being is treated fairly and equally by society and by the government. Injustice toward a single human being is an injustice toward all and an affront to the Almighty God.

Radwan A. Masmoudi, "The Silenced Majority,"
Journal of Democracy, April 2003.

The concept of justice is one of the essential pillars in the maintenance of both the natural and social orders. God, be He Exalted, has said, He has established the scale, therefore, do not transgress in the scale [of justice]. Undertake the measuring with justice and do not cheat concerning the scale. [55:7–8] Justice, as many of our scholars point out, is one of the underpinnings of the order that has been established by God. This reality is also a foundation of a healthy social order. God says in that regard, *O, You who believe! Be upright for*

God, witnesses to justice; and do not let your hatred of a people move you to a position where you are unjust. Be just, that is closer to piety. Be mindful of God! Verily God is well informed concerning all that you do. [Quran 4:135]

This social aspect of justice has been beautifully summarized by Imam al-Qurtubi. He says, discussing the relationship between two words that are usually translated as justice (al-'Adl), and distributive justice (al-Qist), "Justice is the basis of all human relations and a foundation of Islamic rule."[11] This saying is illustrative of the meaning conveyed by the saying of God, *Verily, we have sent Our Messengers with clear proofs, and we have revealed unto them the Scripture and the Balance in order that they lead people with justice. . .* [Quran 57:25]

Imam al-Mawardi has summarized the social implications of distributive justice in the following way:

> One of the things that reforms worldly affairs is the principle of distributive justice. It facilitates amicable relations between people, engenders obedience to the Divine Law, and brings about the prosperity of countries. It is the basis of a thriving economy, strong families, and stable government. Nothing devastates the land nor corrupts the mind as quickly as tyranny. That is because there are no acceptable limits [to regulate tyranny].[12]

For this reason, Ibn Taymiyya sees the responsibilities of Islamic government emanating from a single verse in the Qur'an, *God enjoins that you deliver the Trusts to their rightful possessors. And when you rule over [or judge between] people, that you do so with justice. . .* [Quran 4:58][13] The Noble Prophet has said in this context, "Surely the most beloved of people with God and the closest to Him on the Day of Resurrection will be a just leader. And the most hated of people and the furthest removed from Him will be a tyrannical leader."[14]

Clearing himself from even an inadvertent association with oppressive, unjust acts, our beloved Prophet is reported to have said:

You bring your disputes to me for adjudication; perhaps one of you is less eloquent than another, and I rule against the wronged party on the basis of what I have heard. Therefore, if I inadvertently grant one of you something owed to his brother do not take it, for I am granting him something that constitutes a piece at Hellfire.[15]

Our impeccably just Khalifa 'Umar b. al-Khattab uttered the following penetrating words:

Verily, God sets forth parables for you, and He directs admonition towards you in order that hearts will be quickened. Surely, the hearts are dead until God quickens them. Justice has signs and portents. As for its signs, they are shyness, generosity, humility, and gentleness. As for its portents, they are embodied in mercy. He has [likewise] made for every affair a gate, and He has made that gate accessible by providing a key. The gate of justice is a deep consideration of consequences, and its key is otherworldliness. Consideration of consequences ultimately involves remembering death and preparing for it by freely parting from one's wealth. Otherworldliness involves dealing justly with everyone and being satisfied with what suffices. If one is not satisfied with what suffices him, no abundance will ever enrich him.[16]

Much of this discussion has focused on distributive justice. However, the Qur'an also places great emphasis on commutative justice. God commands us, Do not be moved by partiality to discriminate in meting out divinely legislated punishments. [Quran 24:2] The Prophet Muhammad mentioned that one of the reasons behind the ruination of a nation is a lack of commutative justice.[17] In this context, he mentioned that if his very daughter were to steal, he would not hesitate to punish her to the full extent of the law.[18]

In summary, this brief discussion should make it clear to any Muslim that peace and justice are comprehensive concepts with deep implications and we have to be people committed to peace and justice. We must clearly illustrate to the world that our religion is indeed the religion of peace. However, our striving for peace must never allow us to be unjust, nor should it allow us to passively accept injustices. We must take a stand for justice, as we are ordered in the Qur'an, *Be you upright supporters of justice. . .* [4:135] However, that stand must go far beyond slogans, such as the one mentioned at the beginning of this article, and move into the realm of positive action; action inspired by the Qur'an and the words and deeds of our illustrious Prophet.

Notes

1. This slogan has been particularly popularized by the New York-based activist Rev. Al Sharpton and his followers.

2. Raghib al-Isfahani, al-Mufradat fi Gharib al-Qur'an (Beirut: Dar al Ma'rifa, no date), 239.

3. Al-Isfahani, 239.

4. See The Holy Bible, Isaiah, 9:6–7; and John 14:27.

5. Ibn Hajar al-'Asgalani, Fath al-Bari, 13:369, no. 7321.

6. This Hadith is related by Muslim, Abu Dawud, and at-Tirmidhi in their collections. Quoted in an-Nawawi, Riyaz as-Salihin, 289–290. Ibn Hajar al-'Asgalani, Fath al-Bari, 11:26–27. The full text of the Prophetic Tradition follows: A man asked the Prophet "Which Islam is best?" He replied, "That you provide food, and extend the greeting of peace, to those you know and those you know not."

8. This is the full narration of the Prophetic tradition mentioned in note no.4 above.

9. This meaning is narrated in prophetic traditions that are related by al-Bukhari, Muslim, and Ibn Majah. See for example, Fath al-Bari, 6:599–600. The above quote is the version of Ibn Majah. Al-Bukhari's version mentions that Jesus will "put an end to war."

10. These and other definitions of justice are mentioned in Salih b. 'Abdullah b. Humayd, Nadra an-Na'im fi Makarim Akhlaq ar-Rasul al-Karim (Jeddah: Dar al-Wasila, 2000), 7: 2792.

11. Quoted in Ibn Humayd, Nadr al-Na'im, 8:3153.

12. Quoted in Ibn Humayd, Nadr al-Na'im, 7:2793.

13. See Ahmad b. Taymiyya, As-Siyasa Ash-Shar'iyya (Beirut: Dar al-Afaq alJadida, 1983), 4–5.

14. At-Tirmidhi, no. 1329.

15. Ibn Hajar al-'Asgalani, Fath al-Bari, 5:354.

16. Quoted in ibn Humayd, Nadra an-Na'im, 7:2811.

17. This concept is mentioned at the beginning of the tradition where a lady from Bani Makhzum, one of the most aristocratic Arab tribes, stole something and the companions were moved to intervene for a lessening of her punishment. The Noble Prophet responded, "O people! Those before you were ruined in that if a noble person among them stole something, they left him alone. On the other hand, if a lower class person stole something, they punished him!" See this narration in its entirety in Abi Zakariyya Yahya b. Sharaf an-Nawawi, al-minhaj: Sharh Sahih Muslim (Beirut: Dar at-Ma'rifa, 1419 AH/1998 CE), 11:186-187, no. 4386.

18. An-Nawawi, Al-Minhaj, 11:186–187, no. 4386.

| "The critical distinction between being opposed to American foreign policy in the Muslim World and being anti-American must be maintained."

Western Muslims Must Oppose Islamic Radicalism

M.A. Muqtedar Khan and John L. Esposito

In the viewpoint that follows, M.A. Muqtedar Khan and John L. Esposito contend Muslims in the Western world must take care not to embrace or espouse any extremist rhetoric. While the authors do not advocate censorship, they believe that anti-Western speech can bring only negative repercussions upon Western Muslim communities and further the unfortunate stereotypes that these communities are filled with dangerous radicals. Khan and Esposito insist Muslim communities need to police themselves to ensure criticism does not translate into radicalism. Khan is an associate professor of political science at the University of Delaware. Esposito is a professor of international affairs and Islamic studies at Georgetown University in Washington, D.C.

M.A. Muqtedar Khan and John L. Esposito, "Safe in the West: Western Muslims Should Strive Against Internal Extremism To Ensure Their Safety," Alliance of Civilizations. Reproduced by permission. www.unaoc.org.

As you read, consider the following questions:

1. What do Khan and Esposito see as the three dangers facing Western Muslims today?

2. According to the authors, what are *Juma khutbas*, and how should Western Muslims respond to them?

3. What do the authors fear may happen if radical Muslims in the West continue to demonize the United States and its allies?

The war on terror and its attendant consequences has created extremely difficult circumstances for Muslim Americans, in particular and Western Muslim in general. The changing political and legal environment in Western countries has undermined the quality of life of Western Muslims. Many face workplace discrimination, racial and religious profiling, challenging business environments, travel hassles. The situation has become difficult and risky, and Islamic institutions; particularly mosques and Islamic charities, face harassment and unnecessary scrutiny.

Existential Dangers Face Western Muslims

The challenge for Western Muslims today is existential. If things get worse, what will happen to them? Some fear the rhetoric and recommendations of Islamophobic political commentators questioning the patriotism of Muslim communities in the West and even raising the example of the internment of Japanese Americans during World War II. Clearly the future of Islam and Muslims in the West is at risk, and in this environment Western Muslims will have to manage their politics with foresight, prudence, and patience.

Three potential dangers face Western Muslims.

1. Increased anti-Western terrorism in the Muslim World, which fuels Islamophobia, enhances the political influ-

ence of Western anti-Muslim extremists and enables the institutionalization of legislation designed to undermine the influence of Muslims.

2. The [George W.] Bush administration's foreign policy that is geared towards the projection of American power and reassertion of American hegemony in the Middle East. Aggressive American unilateralism triggers events and actions that ultimately undermine the security and well being of Western Muslims.

3. Homegrown extremism among Muslims.

At the moment, Western Muslims can do little to reduce the first two dangers beyond engaging in dialogues—political and religious—at various levels. However, they can and must play an aggressive and decisive role in eliminating internal extremism that resonates with extremism in the Muslim World. Extremist discourse, actions and postures by a small minority of Western Muslims not only undermine the efforts of the vast majority to improve Western-Islamic relations, they also provide concrete evidence of the most egregious stereotypes of Islam and Muslims.

Countering Inflammatory Discourse

Western Muslim community leaders, activists and scholars must condemn and reject any and all forms of extremist rhetoric coming from Juma khutbas, public statements on TV and other media and from some Muslim publications themselves. Care must be taken to not only moderate Muslim public discourse but also Muslim-Muslim discourse in order to ensure that extremism and vehement anti-Westernism do not take root in the community. Islam and Muslims in the West can be critical of the West and Western ideals but cannot and must not be anti-West. The critical distinction between being opposed to American foreign policy in the Muslim World and being anti-American must be maintained.

In the current environment any criticism of the US foreign policy can be easily construed as anti-Americanism. However, the difficulty of the task does not mean that Muslims should either give up criticism of US policies or embrace anti-Americanism. Consider for example the self-criticism of prominent Western Muslim scholar Tariq Ramadan. He is critical of many Western and Eastern Muslim practices, but in spite of it he is never perceived as un-Islamic or anti-Islamic. Indeed he is embraced by many as an inspirational intellectual. On the other hand Muslim critic such as Irshad Manji is perceived as anti-Islamic by many mainstream Muslims in the US and Canada. Muslims in their criticism of American policies must come across as Tariq Ramadan and not Irshad Manji.

The first thing to achieve this is to eschew blaming the entire American society, or the West or even democracy for the excesses committed by specific administrations or even individuals. For example blaming the entire United States, or 'democracy' or even the West for what happened in Abu Ghraib [where prisoners taken during the 2003 invasion of Iraq were abused by U.S. military police] is akin to blaming Islam for what happened on September 11, 2001 [when suicide pilots crashed planes into the World Trade Center towers]. Often Muslim rhetoric, critical of the US/West, tends to treat the US or the West as monolithic and comes across as anti-Western polemic rather than thoughtful criticism.

The Wrong Things To Say

Most Western Muslims have the same basic desires as many others, material well-being, cultural acceptance and the opportunity to practice their faith without social and political intimidation. Some, however, wish to use their geographic location as an asset in their war against their perceived enemies. The argument made by some, especially the neoconservatives, that radical Islam is well deeply embedded in the West and the Western Muslim community hides in its bosom many se-

The Right Kind of Activism for the U.S. Muslim Community

American Muslims can strengthen their religious activism in cooperation with American Jews and Christians. This means, first, learning from the methods applied by Jewish and Christian activist and charity institutions that do not merely serve their own congregations but dedicate themselves to the greater American good. At the same time, it means developing activities that serve the whole American community, by defending its social, political, and economic freedoms. At the top of the agenda must be assistance to government in directly and forcefully attacking Islamist extremism.

Imaad Malik,
"Islam and Interfaith Relations After 9/11,"
Family Security Matters,
May 3, 2007. www.familysecuritymatters.org.

cret 'sleeper' terrorist cells is patently false. Such claims must be seen as racist and religiously bigoted. No community has been as closely scrutinized as Muslims in America and no widespread threat has been uncovered. The 9/11 Commission fully exonerated the community of any connection to terrorism.

Nevertheless in every Muslim community there is a small group of individuals angry with the West and fearing that Islam is being destroyed. In their anger they say and do counterproductive and dangerous things. Most people in the West are sensible and recognize isolated episodes of violence or intemperate rants. However there are three issues on which a small minority of Western Muslims continues to alienate Western populations from Islam and Muslims.

Justifying suicide bombing: Suicide bombing has become a metaphor for all that is terrible about Islam and Muslims. Even though most Muslims everywhere condemn suicide bombing as un-Islamic some continue to utilize the freedom of speech available in the West to claim that suicide bombing is a noble and Islamically justifiable defense strategy. Such individuals succeed only in branding Islam as a barbaric religion that inspires violence. They also belie the majority of Western Muslims who condemn it and make it look as if they are dissimulating and lying. This promotes the canard that Western Muslims are all secretly supporters of terrorism and that Islam indeed teaches violence.

Equating the war on terror to the war on Islam: Some radical Muslim commentators have been insisting that the war on terror is actually a war on Islam. Unfortunately the history of American foreign policy and recent actions in the Muslim world has convinced many Muslims that the US is at war with Islam. For Western Muslims this is an unacceptable interpretation of what is happening. First of all, it is not true. Islam continues to thrive in the West even today. The prominent role played by Muslims in the 2004 [U.S.] presidential elections is clear proof that in spite of growing Islamophobia and the [U.S.] Patriot Act, they remain a vibrant force and far from being snuffed out. In Europe the presence of Muslims has transformed Europe's foreign policy, its relations with the US and its posture with regards to the Arab-Israeli conflict. Those who insist that the West is at war with Islam do a grave disservice to Western Muslims and also undermine the prospects of future good relations between the West and the Islamic World.

Demonization of the West and democracy: The third theme in radical Muslim discourse includes a rhetorical demonization of the West as evil and democracy as hypocrisy. In a curious way the very existence of this free radical discourse is indicative of how strong democracy is across the board in

Western countries. But this constant demonization of the West (America and Europe), ridicule of their values, icons, religious beliefs, secular beliefs and cultural practices may very well lead to the elimination of free speech and the diminishing of democracy. As far as Western Muslims are concerned, those who attacked the US on 9/11/2001 have caused them untold misery. They cannot allow it to be amplified through irresponsible statements from within their own communities.

The community must get tough on radical discourse. Western Muslims should become more organized and aggressive in marginalizing and condemning voices that justify violence, incite hatred, and practice demonization of the other. How can community members and leaders fight bigots in the mainstream community and the rising Islamophobia if some within their own ranks mirror the same fear, ignorance and prejudice? The struggle for acceptance of Islam and Muslims in the West cannot be divorced from the acceptance of the West within its Muslim communities.

| "A policy of 'neocontainment' would avoid self-defeating military confrontations in favor of an aggressive campaign to isolate our enemies."

The United States Must Contain Islamic Radicalism

Phillip Kapusta and Donovan Campbell

In the following viewpoint, Phillip Kapusta and Donovan Campbell suggest a strategy of containment would be the best U.S. policy for dealing with radical Islam. Recalling this strategy was successful in ending the Cold War, the authors maintain investing in a bulwark of moderate Muslim governments today will keep radicalism at bay until its ideology peters out as communism did in former Eastern bloc countries. Phillip Kapusta is a Navy commander and chief of strategic plans at Special Operations Command Central in Tampa, Florida. Marine Captain Donovan Campbell is a veteran of three combat deployments.

As you read, consider the following questions:

1. Where do Kapusta and Campbell believe the arc of nations with hostile Islamic ideologies extends?

Phillip Kapusta and Donovan Campbell, "How To Contain Radical Islam: The Best Global Strategy for the US May Be the One That Won the Cold War," boston.com, July 27, 2008. Reproduced by permission of the authors.

2. What two countries do the authors single out as worthy of U.S. aid and involvement to expand representative government and economic freedom?

3. What capacities must the military improve upon to meet the demands of the new containment strategy, as outlined by the authors?

The events of [September] 11, 2001, brutally announced the presence of an enemy seemingly distinct from any our country had faced before [when hijackers crashed planes into New York's World Trade Towers]. Unlike previous adversaries, such as Nazi Germany, Imperial Japan, or the Spanish monarchy, this new enemy was difficult to define, let alone understand. It was not motivated by causes that an avowedly secular government could easily comprehend, and it took an amorphous yet terrifying form with little historical precedent.

Our leaders responded to this new threat with dramatic changes. In the largest government reorganization of the past 50 years, the Department of Homeland Security lumbered into existence. A new director of national intelligence was named to oversee America's vast intelligence apparatus, and the defense of the homeland was made the military's top priority. Most dramatically, the United States announced—and then implemented—an aggressive new policy of preemptive war.

Yet, with the seventh anniversary of 9/11 approaching [in 2008], it seems clear that policy makers have not responded particularly well. Islamic extremists are gaining strength, while America finds itself increasingly isolated in the world. The coalition of the willing, never overly robust, is now on life support. In the Middle East, the Islamist parties Hezbollah and Hamas have enough popular support to prosper in free and fair elections [in Palestine], and Al Qaeda is adding franchise chapters in North Africa, the Levant, the Arabian Peninsula, and elsewhere. Our most prominent post-9/11 action remains the Iraq war, which has arguably failed to improve America's national security even as it has strengthened the position of our sworn enemies in the government of Iran.

Looking to an Old Strategy

Underlying these global setbacks is a core problem: The United States has yet to formulate a holistic strategy to guide the prosecution of our new war. We have not articulated a clear set of mutually reinforcing goals, and we have not undertaken a consistent set of actions designed to achieve our aims even as they demonstrate our national values. Indeed, we have not even managed to properly identify our enemies; despite the rhetoric of the past seven years, America is not at war with terror, because terror is not a foe but a tactic.

Blundering forward, we have squandered the swell of global good will after 9/11, punished our friends, and rewarded our enemies with shortsighted, even self-destructive, tactics.

Yet what we face today is not wholly novel: It is a war of ideas, mirroring the Cold War. Like the communists, violent Islamic extremists are trying to spread a worldview that denigrates personal liberty and demands submission to a narrow ideology. And, as with the Cold War, it must be our goal to stop them. The United States should therefore adopt a new version of the policy that served us so well during that last long war: containment.

A policy of "neocontainment" would avoid self-defeating military confrontations in favor of an aggressive campaign to isolate our enemies. The modern equivalent of the Soviet Bloc, that geographic haven for a hostile ideology, is the arc of instability that extends from Central Asia west through Iran and the Arabian Peninsula and south across North Africa. We should build a virtual wall of stable, moderate nations on the periphery of that arc, literally containing the spread of the hostile belief system. More broadly, we must enter into—and prevail in—the war of ideas, winning the hearts and minds of both domestic and foreign audiences. We must pursue this goal not only in the mental arena—in what has been variously describe as political warfare, propaganda, or psychological operations—but also in the practical one, by consistently demonstrating our belief system in action. Our deeds are more important than anything we say, and in the aggressive prosecution of our war on terror, we have strayed from our core value of individual freedom.

The Differences in Today's War

Of course, neocontainment will have to address the important differences between the conflicts of today and yesterday. Today's threat emanates not from a hypergoverned nation-state but from a loosely networked group of radicals based primarily in undergoverned areas of the world—which makes carefully defining and targeting our true foes all the more important. Just as we strove to separate the Soviet elites from the people they repressively ruled, now we must separate the Islamic radicals from the vast majority of Muslims. We cannot, and should not, target an entire religion.

There is also a crucial difference in the danger's scale. For four decades, the USSR [Soviet Union] and its massive nuclear arsenal posed a clear existential threat to the United States. In contrast, today's extremists cannot eliminate our nation. We need to ratchet down the doomsday rhetoric and the military-driven response. Our primary ideological export should not be fear; it should be hope. We are at war with people and their belief systems, and ideas cannot be killed by bullets. They can only be killed by better ideas.

Without a coherent strategy, America's "war on terror" has been tragically inconsistent. We say that our mandate is to spread freedom and democracy, yet we try to do so at the point of a gun. We say that our battle must be fought by a coalition of like-minded allies, but we eschew diplomacy and browbeat our friends when they disagree with us. We say that we stand for the highest human ideals, but the world harbors deep suspicions of our indefinite detentions at Guantanamo [U.S. prison in Cuba for terrorism suspects].

Our contradictory words and actions have alienated virtually the entire Arab world. NATO [North Atlantic Treaty Organization] remains fractured and largely ineffectual against the resurgent Taliban, and the Washington [D.C.] clock has run out on the Iraq war. We have elevated Al Qaeda's importance to nearly our own, and we are moving into a deadly no-man's-land where America is neither respected nor feared. It is almost inconceivable, and yet it has come to this: We are losing the global-influence war to people who blow up women and children at kebab stands.

But if we can retool and take the long view, as the architects of Cold War containment did, we will watch Islamic extremism collapse under the weight of its own contradictions—witness the recent grassroots uprising against Al Qaeda in Iraq. Like Marxism, militant Islam is long on promising the violent overthrow of the materialistic West and short on fashioning actual utopias.

The Containment Doctrine

The original doctrine of containment had its roots in a time of uncertainty much like our own. By the end of World War II, the United States was the dominant global power, and for a brief period there was hope that the world might fashion a lasting peace under the fledgling United Nations.

By 1949, however, it was clear that the world was bifurcating [dividing into two parts] and that this constituted a serious challenge to our security. The Soviet Union became the second nuclear-armed superpower, China fell to communism, and the proliferation of ballistic missiles threatened the American homeland. Coming on the heels of the decisive triumph

The Need To Support Moderate Muslims in the Islamic World

With regard to partners, it will be important [for the United States] to identify the social sectors that would constitute the building blocks of the proposed networks [of moderate Muslims]. Priority should be given to

1. Liberal and secular Muslim academics and intellectuals

2. Young moderate religious scholars

3. Community activists

4. Women's groups engaged in gender equality campaigns

5. Moderate journalists and writers.

The United States should ensure visibility and platforms for these individuals. For example, U.S. officials should ensure that individuals from these groups are included in congressional visits, making them better known to policymakers and helping to maintain U.S. support and resources for the public diplomacy effort.

Assistance programs should be organized around the sectors listed above, and would include

1. *Democratic education,* particularly programs that use Islamic texts and traditions for authoritative teachings that support democratic and pluralistic values

2. *Media.* Support for moderate media is critical to combating media domination by anti-democratic and conservative Muslim elements.

3. *Gender equality.* The issue of women's rights is a major battleground in the war of ideas within Islam, and women's rights advocates operate in very adverse environments. Promotion of gender equality is a critical component of any project to empower moderate Muslims.

4. *Policy advocacy.* Islamists have political agendas, and moderates need to engage in policy advocacy as well. Advocacy activities are important in order to shape the political and legal environment in the Muslim world.

Angel Rabasa, Cheryl Benard, Lowell H. Schwartz, and Peter Sickle, "Building Moderate Muslim Networks," RAND Corporation, 2007.

of the war, the new communist threat generated the same feelings of vulnerability and confusion that the 9/11 attacks would foster decades later.

To respond to this changing world, senior national security officials writing for President Harry Truman articulated a new kind of policy. Drawing heavily from articles written by the American diplomat George Kennan, the landmark National Security Council Report 68 (NSC-68) outlined a strategy of containment that served as the core of American foreign policy for every president from Truman to [Ronald] Reagan.

Presciently, NSC-68 identified the essential clash between the United States and the Soviet Union as one between diametrically opposed ideologies. On the Soviet side was a dogmatic belief system that demanded absolute submission of individual freedom and sought to impose its authority over the rest of the world. On the American side was an ideology premised on the overriding value of freedom, a system founded upon the dignity and worth of the individual. This ideology relied upon its inherent appeal and did not aim to bring other societies into conformity through force of arms.

The policy of containment represented a tectonic shift from the military-centric, unconditional-surrender mentality of World War II. War was now the option of last resort. Coercion through violence represented a contradiction for any free people, and, used improperly, it could undermine the global appeal of the American belief system. Thus, containment did not define success as the military defeat and unconditional surrender of the Soviet regime. It had more modest ambitions: geographic isolation of the communist belief system and slow change over time. By fighting a global struggle for influence, the thinking went, America could avoid a costly full-scale war against the Soviets.

Of course, force was employed on a number of occasions in proxy wars across the globe, such as Vietnam and Korea.

They had serious costs, but compared with a potential all-out war against the USSR, these conflicts remained limited efforts to contain the geographic footprint of the Soviet ideology. And though the American defense budget increased over time, it never became the same drain on our economy that military spending was for the Soviets.

The path dictated by NSC-68 was not a straight line to the collapse of the USSR, but the strategy proved remarkably effective. Communism expanded outside of its containment zone in a few instances, but, for the most part, the United States and its allies successfully implemented the indirect approach recommended by NSC-68. When the once mighty Soviet empire imploded in 1991, it was almost precisely as NSC-68 had predicted.

Building the Right Partnerships

Strikingly, if one replaces "communism" with "Islamic extremism" and "the Kremlin" with "Al-Qaeda," NSC-68 could have been written in 2002, not 1950. Like communism, Islamic extremism lusts for political power, in this case through the restoration of the caliphate and the imposition of Sharia law [Islamic law] on all peoples. Indeed, language from NSC-68 rings eerily true today—it described the Soviets as "animated by a new fanatic faith, antithetical to our own." Al Qaeda and its ilk are the latest in a long line of narrow ideologies that claim to provide the only true answer to life's existential questions. And as with Soviet communism, the idea has a geographic nucleus.

Our task now is to envelop this nucleus with prosperous, stable countries whose inhabitants are free to choose their own beliefs. Working from the outside in, the United States must partner with nations on the periphery to help them build a stronger middle class, enhance their education systems, improve basic health, and lower government corruption. We must help elected and unelected governments to allow greater empowerment of their citizens, whether through a slow march toward representative government or expanded economic opportunity for all classes.

Lebanon in the Middle East and Pakistan in Central Asia are some of the best countries in which to begin and expand this work. In Lebanon's complex political landscape, Iran and Syria support the Islamist Hezbollah party-cum-militia, while the United States backs the secular Lebanese government. Another Islamist movement, Fatah al Islam, enjoys a nebulous connection to Al Qaeda. We should be using our country's massive financial resources to allow the Lebanese government to outspend its competitors by a factor of 10, showering much-needed aid on the Lebanese people, and thus de-legitimizing their opponents and debunking their ideology. Instead, the government cannot meet its basic responsibilities, and extremist movements are increasingly seen as the only institutions capable of bettering lives.

In Pakistan, the extremist cancer in the northwestern provinces continues to grow despite $5.5 billion in direct US military aid. Pakistan's dangerously unstable new civilian government lacks the capability and will to challenge Al Qaeda and the Taliban in the region. Instead of focusing exclusively on military operations along the Afghanistan/Pakistan border, America must broaden its scope to encompass other priorities: tension with India over Kashmir and education reform. Only after a comprehensive Indo/Pakistani border settlement will Pakistan shift its military energy from south to north. In the interim, it will placate us with occasional forays into the frontier provinces, but such adventures will never be decisive. We must also help Pakistan provide a counterweight to the hundreds of Wahhabi madrassas [schools teaching Wahhabi Islam, which is rooted in Saudi Arabia] spreading virulent extremism. As long as these fundamentalist institutions remain the only option for much of the country's poor, Islamic extremists in the tribal areas will enjoy a virtually inexhaustible manpower pool. In the long run, 5,000 secular teachers for Pakistan's middle schools will do more for America's national security than will 50,000 AK-47s for the country's army.

A clear new containment strategy will help us recognize the importance of engaging with such nations at pivotal points before they slide into repressive autocracy (Pakistan in 2001) or all-out chaos (Afghanistan in 1989).

Avoiding Direct Confrontation

It is popular to blame these failings on the attention and resource deficits created by the Iraq war. But they are just as much the result of the black-and-white mentality that governs our approach to foreign affairs—liberal democracy or nothing. In working with periphery states, we must be willing to accept outcomes that are less than perfect. Indeed, we must be willing to accept ruling regimes that may not like us at all. We are not trying to create mini-Americas scattered across the globe; we are looking to foster stable, free countries whose people will have little interest in the repressive ideology of our enemies.

On occasion, extremist governments hostile to the existence of the United States (Hamas in the Gaza Strip) will enjoy broad popular support, but preemptive wars must become a thing of the past. We cannot say that we value freedom and then seek political change through force when the choice of the people produces regimes not to our liking. However, the military can, and must, be used to target individuals bent on terror aimed at American interests. Furthermore, if a nation enables attacks on our homeland, as Afghanistan did under the Taliban, then we must use all necessary means to defend ourselves. On rare occasions, this will require full-out war and postinvasion reconstruction.

Retrospectively, the neocontainment framework would have supported operations in Afghanistan. It is a country near the edge of the arc, and its then-rulers harbored extremists who had demonstrated the motive and means to substantially damage our nation. Compared with our original plan, though, neocontainment would have stressed the importance of dominating the postcombat phase by committing all implements of national power to the years of sustained effort required to rebuild Afghanistan.

In contrast, neocontainment would have argued against the invasion of Iraq. Allocating the same amount of effort and resources to bolstering nations ringing the region would have produced far more beneficial results than invading a country at its heart. By doing so, our actions strengthened the extremist narrative that there is a Western crusade against Islam, and Iran's Shia theocracy has been the biggest beneficiary of the power vacuum left by Saddam's demise.

Going forward, adopting a strategy of neocontainment will entail checking Iran's expansion efforts through proxies rather than direct strikes against the country itself. Just as we limited Soviet expansion without using overt force against the Warsaw Pact, so too can we contain the Iranian regime without flying B-2s over Tehran.

The War of Ideas Is Most Important

Furthermore, we must institutionalize the lessons learned so painfully over seven years of war. The military must dramatically improve its nation-building doctrine, capacity, and will, acknowledging that postwar stability is much more important in the long run than is dominating the active combat phase. We remain unchallenged in our ability to win conventional military conflicts, but we must develop the language skills, cultural awareness, and civil-affairs specialists necessary to prevail in unconventional campaigns and in fighting's messy aftermath.

Our next president [in 2009] will inherit a nation weary of war, a world skeptical of American motives and actions, and undecided conflicts in Iraq and Afghanistan. However, the energy and excitement of a government transition offer both the outgoing and incoming administrations the opportunity to take bold steps.

On the battlefield, it is at least as important to articulate what you are for as it is to define what you are against. In a war of ideas, this is even more critical. To do this across the world, nation by nation, will take time, and that does not come naturally to our fast paced, results-oriented society. But we need to muster the requisite patience. Untold numbers of lives hinge on it.

| "I believe this century will be remembered as the one in which Islam began its long march to extinction."

Islam Will Fall and Be Forgotten

Alan Caruba

Alan Caruba is a business and science writer and the founder of the National Anxiety Center, an organization that takes issue with the way national interest topics are portrayed in the media. In the following viewpoint, Caruba contends Islam is a corrupt religion that advocates death over peace and exclusion over inclusion. After noting the views of disgruntled ex-Muslims, Caruba asserts many adherents will ultimately reject Islam and the religion will simply disappear in time.

As you read, consider the following questions:

1. To what past regime does Caruba compare Islam and its advocacy of jihad?

2. As Caruba explains, what are *dhimmis*, and how does he use them to further his argument?

Alan Caruba, "The Decline and Fall of Islam," TYSK: Thought You Should Know, June 5, 2003. Reproduced by permission. www.tysknews.com.

3. What does the author believe is a "hopeful sign" in the war to end the dream of Islamic domination of the world?

None of us will live to see it, but before this millennium is over, Islam is likely to have joined the myths of ancient Egypt, Greece and Rome as a religion that was tested and failed.

The violence being visited upon the world by al Qaeda [terrorist organization] and other Islamic fundamentalists cannot survive a "holy war" against America and the West. Jihad's chosen instrument—terror—did not save communism from its failure in the last century's police state of the Soviet Union and it will not save Islam in the Middle East and elsewhere.

If anything, the Jihad is the ultimate expression of the failure of Islam, a religion conjured up by Muhammad in the seventh century of Christendom. The year ascribed to its birth is AD 622. There are an estimated 1.2 billion Muslims around the world, mostly in the Middle East, Africa, and Asia, but there are more than 31 million in Europe, over a million and a half in South America, and at least 2.9 million in America.

The religion is divided between its Sunni and Shiite branches, but there is a deep divide as well in the hearts of an unknown number of Muslims, many of whom have concluded it ill-serves humanity in general and their own lives in particular. Some believe that Islam and democracy can be compatible. I doubt this because its history is one of monarchy and autocracy.

A Barbarous Religion

Edited by Ibn Warraq, *Leaving Islam: Apostates Speak Out* is an impressive collection of views by former Muslims, many of whom must still remain anonymous because Islam prescribes death to any apostate. *Why I Am Not A Muslim* is Warraq's

Intellectuals Desert Islam

I know many of you are pessimistic about it but I foresee the end of Islam in sight. I am not concerned about the ignorant mass of Muslims. The intellectuals of Islam are turning against it and it is the intellectuals that chart the course of the history not the ignorant mass. A billion ignorant Muslims can do nothing to stop the momentum that a few of their enlightened intellectuals who have turned against Islam can generate. They eventually will have to give in and follow their intellectuals or they will be annihilated under the pressure of poverty like Afghanistan and Iran.

Many Muslim intellectuals feel that they have hit the bottom and even though they still are unable to out their umbilical cord from Islam, they admit that Islam cannot bring prosperity, democracy and peace and they openly call for the separation of Mosque from State. This admission that Islam has failed, at least in political front, is a great step forward. Whether these people are aware or not, they are tacitly acknowledging that Islam is a failed paradigm; because Islam unlike Christianity, Hinduism or Buddhism is a religion that seeks power and pretends to be the religion of the state. Islam becomes meaningless once it is reduced into a mere set of moral codes. Islam has very few moral codes. The essence of Islam is to fight and promote the religion of Allah until it becomes the sole religion of mankind. Without this expansionist drive, Islam will wither and die.

Ali Sina,
"The Fall of Islam," Faith Freedom International,
August 2001. www.faithfreedom.org.

scholarly examination of Islam that reveals that it is little more than a barbarous cult based on the life of Muhammad. Both are worth reading.

As noted, rejecting Islam to accept another faith or even to become an atheist brings with it the threat of death. It is the mark of a religion that believes any deviation from its dogma gives it the right to kill in order to justify itself. Until the Reformation transformed Christianity, it too meted out death to apostates and unbelievers. But this is the year AD 2003 and in free societies, one's religion is not a concern of the state. Under Islam, the religion is the state. In Muslim nations, the Koran and sharia law [Islamic law] derived from it is the only law.

While Islam has permitted "dhimmis", non-Muslims, to live in Islamic nations, in practice their "protection" has been non-existent. It was and is dangerous to be anything other than a Muslim in such places. Islam, by its very nature seeks to dominate all who come under its control and deeply resents those who will not convert.

The Views of Former Muslims

Brief excerpts from Warraq's books provide instant insight why Islam stands on shifting sands. Written between February 2001 and April 2002, here are some posts from the Internet site Warraq maintains (www.secularislam.org). There is considerable irony in the way those who choose to reject Islam did so, as often as not, because they read its holy book, the Koran.

> The biggest flaw of the Koran is what is not in it. There are many crimes a person can commit; yet the Koran mentions only the punishments for a mere three or four. I was astonished at the fact that the Koran mentions nothing about punishment for rape. The word "rape" is not even mentioned once in the Koran, as if it were not worth bringing up.

Muhammad took many wives, but many Muslims are appalled by the story of Aisha, a child whose age is debated within Islam as being as young as six but no more than nine years of age. "How can a man of more than fifty years have sexual feelings for a girl of only six?" asked a Pakistani who went on to ask, "Why is it that a woman is lower than a man? Is my mother lower than me? Why is it that a Muslim man can have four wives? And why did Muhammad have more than four wives?" He concluded, "Islam is just the ramblings of some delusioned Arab madman."

Yet another says, "I could not remain a Muslim because Islam hates women. Islam says that women are inferior in every way. What sort of religion forces fathers to make their daughters suffer? Islam has no joy. Islam is a cult of tears and death."

A Guide to War

While Warraq's book is literally filled with such personal revelations by those either raised as Muslims or converts to it, I will conclude with a view expressed by a former Muslim who, upon reading the Koran, said, "I became very worried by the amount of violence in it. Subsequent late-night sessions with the Koran convinced me that I was reading a guide to war."

The Koran is a guide to war. Thievery was the way Muhammad supported himself as the self-proclaimed prophet and conquest was the way Muhammad and his followers initially spread Islam. The United States, a target and a victim in this Jihad, is waging war to end the Islamic dream of domination. In this it has been joined by many nations, including those that are Islamic. This should be seen as a hopeful sign.

I believe this century will be remembered as the one in which Islam began its long march to extinction. It will be defeated in its terror war and it will be defeated because many will abandon a "religion" that is repelled by modernity, denies human rights, and revels in the blood of its victims, calling their killers martyrs.

| *"The West appears to be doomed with
or without Islam."*

Both Islam and the West Will Fall

Mumin Salih

In the viewpoint that follows, Mumin Salih, an ex-Muslim from the Middle East, claims both Islam and the West will decline and fall in the future. Salih insists the rigid mind control of Islamic elites will be broken by the Internet and other global forces that will allow common Muslims to see they are victims of misguided and dangerous beliefs. But according to Salih, this realization will come too late to aid the West, which has not taken the threat of radical Islam seriously enough to protect itself. Salih maintains the West is not championing its own culture and is too easily willing to surrender its cultural dominance rather than take pride in its achievements and supremacy.

As you read, consider the following questions:

1. How has Islam "guarded its ideology," according to Salih?

2. In Salih's view, why are today's Westerners reluctant to defend freedom and democracy?

Mumin Salih, "Islam Will Lose, So Will the West," Islam Watch, February 16, 2008. Reproduced by permission. www.islam-watch.org.

3. In the author's opinion, what is blinding Westerners to the virtues of their countries and the achievements of their culture?

Islam is currently passing through one of its most dynamic times since its rise fourteen-hundred years ago. This dynamic period started long before 9/11 [the terrorist attacks on September 11, 2001, in the United States] as a fierce struggle, mainly against the West, but also against any nation or group that dares to stand in its way. Most Muslims take this resurgence phase very seriously and consider it as a decisive battle between Islam and the non-Islam, or the kufr, which Mohammed told them they would win. Even though the West, currently, is largely in denial about this makes no difference to the significance of this conflict to the whole world.

Islam Tolerates No Criticism

Virtually unchallenged, Islam has survived and expanded during the last fourteen centuries. The only time Islam had ever faced any challenges was in the first few years, when Mohammed's claims of being a prophet, were questioned by the Meccan Arabs and then by the Jews of Yathrib. During that period, which spanned over thirteen years, Mohammed failed to win any intellectual debate to prove his claims. That reflected on Mohammed's failure to attract genuine followers. The few dozen who joined him were mainly friends and beneficiaries. Once Mohammed established his stronghold in Yathrib, which he renamed as Medina, intellectual debates, which had flourished until few years before his arrival, became meaningless and virtually non-existent. Since then, the only challenges Islam ever had were military ones; the opposing forces were more interested in military conquests than in exposing Islam's ideology.

Knowing the Muslims' mindset, we can safely say that Muslims may not even bother to consider any critical analysis of Islam that comes from non-Muslims, no matter how genuine and legitimate it may be. If Muslims ever mention such painstaking and authentic works, it is only to dismiss them as the works of the enemy of Islam. On the other hand, the critical analysis of Islam that comes from Muslims is often taken more seriously, although those Muslim critics of Islam will be branded as infidels.

Islam has guarded its ideology by employing a thorough indoctrination program and systematic and extensive brainwashing process of its adherents. The process is so incapacitating that it is incomprehensible to Muslims to contemplate their existence outside their religion.

Over the past fourteen centuries, Islam was never openly challenged or critiqued, because those who knew about its myths, also knew what it meant to disclose them. Those Muslims who did their own critical appraisal of their religion kept their results to themselves since they knew if they didn't they risk losing their heads by the authorities, or even by family members or friends who would be happy to do it for the sake of Allah.

A Modern Enlightenment Will Break Islam's Bonds

Even during the last few centuries, when the whole world started to open up to a new age of enlightenment, Islamic authorities managed to seal the minds of Muslims towards any outside views about Islam. The tight seal on the Muslims' minds continues even during our time. Unwanted materials, whether printed or televised, are simply filtered out. For fourteen centuries, Muslims never had a chance to see their religion from any perspective other than their own. Islam survived because it always had a suitable environment of darkness and one-way coaching with no tolerance to different views.

Since the introduction of the Internet all that has changed. Thanks to the power of the Internet, the world is now open to

Defending a Dangerous Religion

The benevolent nature of [friendly Western] Muslims has a profound psychological effect on Westerners. It causes us to say, "Wait a minute. Islam can't be bad, because Muslims are such nice people. Thus, the terrorists who blow up buildings and subways must be *extremists.*" Once we have convinced ourselves of this, we may even find ourselves defending Islam, as I once did. We know that people are angry at terrorists, and we know that some of these angry people may want to take out their anger on Muslims. So we end up defending Islam in order to protect our Muslim friends. While protecting people is certainly a noble goal, defending Islam is an entirely different story. . . .

I'm very happy that most Muslims are willing to live in peace with their neighbors. Yet we have to be honest here. Benevolent Muslims aren't peaceful because they are following the example set by Muhammad. They are peaceful because they've chosen to do what's right, and because they are willing to live far better lives than Muhammad himself lived.

David Wood,
"The Two Faces of Islam . . . Still Smiling,"
Answering Islam: A Christian Muslim Dialog,
July 7, 2005. www.answering-islam.org.

almost everyone, and Muslims can have access to the alternative views about Islam, something considered impossible in the past. The Internet is the first true challenge to Islam because it breaks through all the Islamic security systems. The Internet doesn't recognize Islam's demands of submission and total surrender of the mind. Everything about Islam is now subjected to critical scrutiny, people now ask logical questions and demand logical answers. Every day, the Internet sheds more light on the cult of darkness to expose its myths. This shakes the very foundation of the Islamic ideology. Muslims are slow to come out from the darkness, which is understandable, considering their programmed state of mind. They behave like the battery chickens that are so conditioned to the darkness that when they see the light they feel scared to come out. We are only in the beginning of the Internet age, the process may appear to be slow, but the ball started rolling and more Muslims will wake up to the light of truth and come out to the world of enlightenment and join the other ex-Muslims in exposing the myths of Islam.

The West Is in Decline

I sincerely hope that time will prove me wrong on this gloomy prediction, but the signs are that the West is already losing. It did not take more than one generation for the Western nations, which emerged victorious after WWII [World War II], to lose their momentum and give up any hope of staying in the lead. I write this part of the [viewpoint] with Britain in mind because it seems to be leading the way, but other countries are not far behind.

The decline of the West is mainly an endogenous problem that neither Islam nor any other external factors can be blamed for. But it is a disturbing observation that the West appears to be doomed with or without Islam, although Islam is taking advantage of the process and is working hard to speed it up. The Islamic predators look at the West as a helpless prey and are closing in waiting for the right moment to make a kill. They are hopeful to inherit the West without even having to fight for it, and they do not make a secret of it. A few years ago, [Libya's leader] colonel [Muammar al-] Ghaddafi said that Muslims couldn't take Europe by force in the past, but now they will take it without force. If you don't believe the

Libyan leader's remarks, you only need to visit a classroom in a British primary school to see how Britain will look like in the future.

Nations behave like individuals because they are made of individuals. An individual's performance is at its best in times of stress like preparing for exams or entering competitions. Nations too perform best in times of stress like wars or other national struggles. During the last war, the Western nations' performance was at its peak. People took no chances; they went through some rough times, suffered of hardship, fought wars and lost lives to secure a good future for their children and grandchildren. Those children and grandchildren are today's Westerners who have reaped the fruits of their grandfathers' hard work. Today's Westerners enjoy a freedom and democracy that they never earned and seem to be reluctant to defend.

The West Ignores the Threat of Islam

The West had some very painful experiences because of Islam, like the attacks of 9/11 and the bombings in Madrid [in 2004] and London [in 2006] to mention only few. We all hate painful experiences, but it seems that pain is essential to the survival of individuals as well as nations. It is the uncomfortable sensation of pain that makes a man move away when he sits on a sharp object, otherwise he would bleed to death. It is the uncomfortable sensation of pain that alarms the sufferer to go and seek treatment for its cause. Pain is a warning system that alarms people about the more serious underlying problems that need attention. However, there are people who are careless enough, or stupid enough, not to take action other than swallowing painkillers until they succumb to their ailment.

The bombing of Western targets all over the world during the last few decades should have been enough to motivate the West to take action about the roots of the problem, which we all know to be Islam. Instead, the West has opted to taking

painkillers in the form of politically correct justifications pre-
scribed to them by the politically correct groups. I am afraid
that is a recipe for disaster.

Westerners' Weaknesses

The Western societies seem to have an inherent serious problem that makes the Westerners turn against their own history,
heritage, culture and all their past achievements. They happily
declare their cultural surrender as they see everything coming
from the outside as genuine and honest, and look down at
their own as false and corrupt. They are so consumed with
post imperial guilt that they are blinded to their countries' virtues.

The weakness in the West plays well in the hands of the
Islamists and hinders our campaign to enlighten Muslims and
defeat their cult. Western converts to Islam are used by the
Islamists' propaganda machine to boost the Muslims' confi-
dence in their religion. It is a common observation that when
Muslims run out of answers to defend the Islamic myths, they
produce the most bizarre reason for staying with Islam, they
say: "but all those Westerners wouldn't convert unless Islam is
right".

The West has been a safe haven to the radical Islamic organizations that are banned in their own Islamic countries.
The Western social and political system facilitated some of the
most notorious Islamic organizations, to survive, thrive and
terrorize the innocents around the world. The remarks made
by the head of the Anglican Church about introducing sharia
law [Islamic law] to Britain are just another reminder that the
British problem is largely a self-inflicted one. The response of
the British people to their problems is disappointing to say
the least. Those who recognize the problem leave everything
and emigrate, while the rest turn a blind eye and live in de-

nial. I am afraid that when the nation's feelings are so numbed, it is unlikely that it will sense any threat or react decisively to any danger.

Periodical Bibliography

The following articles have been selected to supplement the diverse views presented in this chapter.

Ali Mohamed al-Damkhi   "Environmental Ethics in Islam: Principles, Violations, and Future Perspectives," *International Journal of Environmental Studies*, February 2008.

Andrew Anthony   "The Future of Islam," *Salon*, October 12, 2004. www.salon.com.

Edwin Anthony   "Muslims and Globalization," *I-MAG*, Summer 2007.

Mark Juergensmeyer   "Islam and the Secular State: Negotiating the Future of Shari'a," *Christian Century*, September 9, 2008.

Daniel Pipes   "Islam's Future," *New York Post*, August 13, 2002.

Bill Powell   "Struggle for the Soul of Islam," *Time*, September 13, 2004.

Carla Power   "Breaking Through," *Time*, January 30, 2008.

———   "Halal Goes Global," *New Statesman*, June 5, 2008.

Atta-ur-Rahman and Anwar Nasim   "Time for 'Enlightened Moderation,'" *Nature*, November 18, 2004.

Aisha Stacey   "Muslims: Citizens of the World," *Islamic Magazine*, Summer 2007.

Mark Steyn   "The Silence of the Artistic Lambs," *Maclean's*, December 3, 2007.

For Further Discussion

Chapter 1

1. After reading the viewpoints in this chapter, think about ideals traditionally associated with the West, such as democracy, capitalism, freedom of speech, and liberty, to name a few. Do you believe that these institutions and their accompanying values are unique to Western society, or do all humans possess the inherent desire to be free from tyranny and to dictate their own future, as suggested by Anwar Ibrahim? Is the religion of Islam and its teachings oppressing people, or are dictators distorting the religion in order to retain their positions of power and control? Use examples from the viewpoints to support your claims.

2. After reading this chapter, do you feel the United States has been drawn into a needlessly long war against terror because it refuses to acknowledge Islam as the root of terror? Or, is it wrong to place such a strong focus on Islam? Is it useless for the United States to promote democracy in Muslim countries because there are fundamental differences between Islamic and democratic values that will ultimately render democratic governments incapable of functioning there? Or, has the United States' method of democracy promotion been flawed from the start? Conduct further research as needed to support your views.

Chapter 2

1. Richard Warren Field argues that by vilifying the religion of Islam, moderate Muslims will feel alienated and unable to fully commit to the fight against radical Islam and terrorism. Justine A. Rosenthal contends that treating all

Muslim terrorists as Islamic radicals with the goal of establishing a global Islamic state ignores the fact that many Muslim terrorists seek only to achieve nationalistic goals; she believes this grouping could potentially encourage nationalist and international terrorists to join forces. After reading both viewpoints, do you believe that it is more important to distinguish between moderate and radical Muslims or to differentiate between nationalist and internationalist Muslim terrorists? Are both views equally important in the fight to defeat terrorism on a global scale? What fundamental misunderstandings of Islam and Islamic terrorism are highlighted by the authors? Explain your answer using information from both viewpoints.

2. Reread the viewpoints in this chapter and conduct some further research into the religion of Islam. Based on the information you find, decide whether you believe Islam to be a violent or peaceful religion. After forming your view, go back and look critically at the sources you have read. Are they Western sources or Islamic sources? How do you think the authors' background might influence their view of Islam and the viewpoint they have taken on the religion? Do you find any evidence that the Western media tends to portray Islam as violent? Of the viewpoints in this chapter, do the Western authors take a more negative view of Islam than the Muslim authors, or are both groups of authors able to objectively assess the facts about the religion and make a judgment based solely on fact? Finally, decide what role, if any, you believe your own upbringing and experiences have played in your definition of Islam as violent or peaceful.

Chapter 3

1. Ruqaiyyah Waris Maqsood argues that many of the restrictions placed on women in Islamic societies have nothing to do with religious teaching but instead are imposed

solely by capricious governments. She avows that the Qur'an places very modest boundaries on the conduct and dress of women and explicitly accepts that women and men are moral equals. Do you think Maqsood's testimonial is convincing or is the indictment by Robert Spencer and Phyllis Chesler more believable in terms of Islam's treatment of women? Use citations from the viewpoints to explain or refute the evidence given.

2. Syed Kamran Mirza claims that honor killings will always be associated with Muslim families because of specific Islamic views about adultery and fornication. He explicitly states that honor killings "is different from other killings" in this respect. Robert Wagner, on the other hand, claims that "honor killings are a global phenomenon and not isolated to Muslims" because they happen in other cultures. How do you think honor killings should be treated if they are to be addressed—as cultural violence, domestic violence, or some other category of violence? Defend your answer using excerpts from the viewpoints.

3. From the examples given in this chapter, choose one limitation placed on women in Islamic society that you think should be redressed before all others. Explain why you believe this restriction or incidence of oppression merits such an immediate remedy. What do you think would be the hoped-for consequence of making this change?

Chapter 4

1. Abdel-Wahab Elmessiri writes that "the West is not hostile to Islam, per se. It is hostile to a resistant Islam, an Islam that challenges the West's Darwinism and consumerism." Do you agree with Elmessiri's contention that the West has an antagonistic relationship with Islam because Islamic nations are not willing to quietly resign themselves to "the cage of ever spiralling production and consumption for the sole purpose of material comfort and worldly

pleasure"? Explain what role you believe rapacious consumerism does or does not play in the conflict between East and West.

2. M.A. Muqtedar Khan and John L. Esposito argue that "the struggle for acceptance of Islam and Muslims in the West cannot be divorced from the acceptance of the West within its Muslim communities." After reading their viewpoint, do you think Khan and Esposito are asking too much of Muslim communities in the West? Explain what parts of their viewpoint you agree with and what parts—if any—you find troubling. In answering this question, make clear what demands or requests you would make upon Muslim leaders in the West during the protracted war on terror.

3. Consider the viewpoints of Alan Caruba and Mumin Salih. Do you find their arguments convincing concerning the eventual fall of Islam? Explain what aspects of their arguments you agree with and/or to which you strongly object. If you agree that Islam is destined to collapse, do you believe other religions will share the same fate for the same reasons Caruba and Salih give? Why or why not?

Organizations to Contact

The editors have compiled the following list of organizations concerned with the issues debated in this book. The descriptions are derived from materials provided by the organizations. All have publications or information available for interested readers. The list was compiled on the date of publication of the present volume; the information provided here may change. Be aware that many organizations take several weeks or longer to respond to inquiries, so allow as much time as possible.

ACT! for America
P.O. Box 6884, Virginia Beach, VA   23456
e-mail: info@actforamerica.org
Web site: www.actforamerica.org

Founded by a Lebanese immigrant to the United States, ACT! for America seeks to provide a voice of opposition to Islamic radicalism and terror. Founder Brigitte Gabriel believes political correctness has stifled honest discussion about the authoritarianism inherent in Islamofacism and the fundamental differences between these ideals and those of the West. Gabriel seeks, through her organization, to provide a critical voice to the discussion and explain why the West must actively oppose the influence of fundamentalist Islam. Articles and information about the organization's current campaigns can be found on the ACT! for America Web site.

American Enterprise Institute (AEI)
1150 Seventeenth St. NW, Washington, DC   20036
(202) 862-5800 • fax: (202) 862-7177
Web site: www.aei.org

The conservative organization AEI promotes the conservative principles of limited government, private enterprise, individual liberty, and vigilant national defense and foreign policies. Institute fellows report on issues of importance to U.S. foreign policy; specific to Islam, AEI has enlisted the services of Ayaan Hirsi Ali, a native of Somalia who became a citizen of the Netherlands in 1992 and served in Dutch parliament from 2003 to 2006. Ali writes extensively about the relationship between Islam and the West as well as the rights of women in Islam. Other AEI fellows have addressed the role of Islam in the Middle East region as a whole, and the relationship between Islam and the West. *The American* is the bimonthly magazine of AEI; articles from this publication as well as other reports and op-eds can be accessed from the AEI Web site.

The American Muslim (TAM)
e-mail: tameditor@aol.com
Web site: www.theamericanmuslim.org

TAM was a quarterly print journal founded in 1989 to promote Muslim culture and provide articles and analysis of Islam and society. The magazine ceased publication in 1995 but was revived in the wake of the September 11, 2001, terrorist attacks to rekindle debate and cross cultural understanding and to provide a voice for moderate Muslims in a discussion that often focuses on radical Islam. Articles on the Web site are categorized by topic such as education, educating about Islam, interfaith issues, and the clash/dialogue of civilizations.

Brookings Institution
1775 Massachusetts Ave. NW, Washington, DC 20036
(202) 797-6000
e-mail: communications@brookings.edu
Web site: www.brookings.edu

The Brookings Institution conducts independent research to construct policy recommendations to strengthen U.S. democracy, guarantee social and economic security and opportunity for all U.S. citizens, and facilitate stable and open international relations. Brookings scholars have directly addressed the prominence of Islam worldwide and have written articles analyzing the relationship between Islam and the West, the role of Islam in terrorism, and the treatment of women in Islamic nations. Brookings has also focused directly on connections between the United States and Islam with its initiative "U.S. Relations with the Islamic World." Articles covering these topics and more can be accessed from the Brookings Institution Web site.

Center for Cross Cultural Understanding

P.O. Box 724, Dalton, GA   30720
e-mail: editor@ccun.org
Web site: www.ccun.org

Established in May 2007 by Dr. Hassan El-Najjar, the Center for Cross Cultural Understanding seeks to encourage world peace through an increased knowledge and acceptance of cultures foreign to one's own. El-Najjar publishes articles explaining the beliefs of Islam for individuals not familiar with the religion and provides a viewpoint to counter the one traditionally produced regarding the wars in Palestine, Iraq, and Afghanistan. These articles, as well as others from the Center's predecessor, Al-Jazeerah, can be accessed online.

Center for Strategic and International Studies (CSIS)

1800 K St. NW, Washington, DC
(202) 887-0200 • fax: (202) 775-3199
Web site: www.csis.org

CSIS is dedicated to providing policy suggestions after researching and analyzing issues relating to defense and security policy, global problems, and regional studies. The center hosts the Congressional Forum on Islam to foster debate and discussion between scholars of Islam and government policy makers. In addition, CSIS has published books such as *Modernization; Democracy and Islam; Islam and Human Rights*; and *Islam, Europe's Second Religion* that explore the impact of Islam worldwide. The *Washington Quarterly* is the official publication of the center.

Council on Foreign Relations (CFR)
The Harold Pratt House, 58 East 68th St.
New York, NY   10065
(212) 434-9400 • fax: (212) 434-9800
Web site: www.cfr.org

The nonpartisan, membership organization CFR provides information and insight on current foreign policy issues in the United States through its backgrounders, roundtables, study groups, and reports. CFR does not take any official position on the issues; its publications present balanced views of the topics and provide a starting point for continued debate. The council has addressed a wide range of subjects relating to Islam in its publications with titles such as: *Islam: Governing Under Sharia; Middle East: Islam and Democracy*; and *Women in Islam. Foreign Affairs* is the bimonthly magazine published by the council.

Heritage Foundation
214 Massachusetts Ave. NE, Washington, DC   20002-4999
(202) 546-4400
e-mail: info@heritage.org
Web site: www.heritage.org

As a conservative think tank, the Heritage Foundation works to preserve the principles of limited government, free-market economics, and a strong national defense in the United States. The organization has explored the impact of Islam on current international affairs through forums, such as Notions of Liberty in Islam, gathering experts to discuss related topics. Additionally, scholars at the foundation have testified before Congress and written extensively on the increasing prominence of Islam and its compatibility with Western values. Transcripts, audio, and video of these events as well as copies of these publications can be accessed from the foundation's Web site.

Middle East Forum (MEF)
1500 Walnut St., Suite 1050, Philadelphia, PA   19102
(215) 546-5406 • fax: (215) 546-5409

e-mail: info@meforum.org
Web site: www.meforum.org

MEF believes the Middle East constitutes an ongoing problem for the United States and works to provide a definitive role for U.S. involvement in the region. The forum advocates for a policy that fights radical Islam, improves democratization efforts, and advances the study of the Middle East in the United States. Articles on the Web site are organized by topic, including Islam, radical Islam, and democracy and Islam. MEF's official publication is *Middle East Quarterly*.

Middle East Policy Council (MEPC)
1730 M St. NW, Suite 512, Washington, DC   20036
e-mail: info@mepc.org
Web site: www.mepc.org

Since 1981, the MEPC has been providing political analysis of issues relating specifically to the Middle East and fostering ongoing debate and education by sponsoring conferences for educators and government officials. Articles and events sponsored by the organization often focus on the relationship between current issues in the Middle East and Islam. The quarterly journal *Middle East Policy* is the organization's official publication; articles from this publication as well as other reports can be read on the MEPC Web site.

Minaret of Freedom Institute
4323 Rosedale Ave., Bethesda, MD   20814
(301) 907-0947
e-mail: mfi@minaret.org
Web site: www.minaret.org

The Minaret of Freedom Institute works to educate both Muslims and non-Muslims to promote greater understanding and acceptance between the two groups. For non-Muslims, the institute's goal is to counter misinformation about Islam by providing the compatibility between Islam and modern values and to advance the status of Muslim people. For Muslims, the institute seeks to educate the community about the benefits of free markets and liberty and to promote free trade and justice as a common interest of both Islam and the West. Articles about Islamic society, women in Islam, civil liberties, and others can be read on the institute's Web site.

Muslim Council of Britain (MCB)

P.O. Box 57330, London   E1 2WJ
England
+44 (0) 845 262 6786 • fax: +44 (0) 207 247 7079
e-mail: admin@mcb.org.uk
Web site: www.mcb.org.uk

MCB is an umbrella organization for more than 500 national, regional, and local organizations, mosques, charities, and schools. The council works to unite these groups to foster cooperation and participation to achieve betterment of society. Additionally, the organization works to promote a more complete understanding of Islam through its publications, projects, and events. The MCB provides an online library of articles, fact sheets, and reports.

New York University Center for Dialogues: Islamic World—U.S.—The West

194 Mercer St., 4th Floor, New York, NY   10012
(212) 998-8693 • fax: (212) 995-4091
e-mail: info@centerfordialogues.org
Web site: www.centerfordialogues.org

Founded following the terrorist attacks of September 11, 2001, the Center for Dialogues seeks to foster communication between and about the Islamic World, the United States, and the West as a whole. Conferences sponsored by the institute focus on topics such as the misunderstandings between the West and the Islamic world, Muslims in the West, and the role of other institutions, such as the media and education, in shaping perceptions. Reports published by the center such as *Muslim Youth and Women in the West: Source of Concern or Source of Hope?* and *Who Speaks for Islam? Who Speaks for the West?* can be read online.

Project on Middle East Democracy (POMED)
P.O. Box 25533, Washington, DC   20027-8533
(202) 422-6804
Web site: www.pomed.org

POMED was founded to assess methods of developing democracies in the Middle East and to analyze how the United States can foster this development. The organization has addressed many of the questions of whether Islam and democracy are compatible and has published numerous articles exploring the similarities between the two and examining what changes need to be made in the Middle East to advance democracy further. Additionally, POMED has addressed general questions concerning Islam in articles such as "Who Will Speak for Islam?" and "Myth of Moderate Islam?" Articles and reports by POMED scholars can be read online.

Washington Institute for Near East Policy
1828 L St. NW, Suite 1050, Washington, DC   20036
(202) 452-0650 • fax: (202) 223-5364
Web site: www.washingtoninstitute.org

The Washington Institute for Near East Policy works to advance an understanding of the relationship between the United States and the Middle East as a region and promote active engagement between the two. Research areas focus on individual countries in the region as well as on larger issues such as U.S. policy in the region and the impact of Islam on interactions between the Middle East and the West. Reports on these issues and others can be read online.

Bibliography of Books

Saleemah
Abdul-Ghafur
Living Islam Out Loud: American Muslim Women Speak. Boston: Beacon, 2005.

Ayaan Hirsi Ali
The Caged Virgin: An Emancipation Proclamation for Women and Islam. New York: Free Press, 2006.

Kecia Ali and
Oliver Leaman
Islam: The Key Concepts. New York: Routledge, 2008.

Tawfiq Alsaif
Islamic Democracy and Its Limits: The Iranian Experience since 1979. London: Saqi, 2007.

Mohammed
Ayoob
The Many Faces of Political Islam: Religion and Politics in the Muslim World. Ann Arbor, MI: University of Michigan Press, 2008.

Paul M. Barrett
American Islam: The Struggle for the Soul of a Religion. New York: Farrar, Straus and Giroux, 2007.

Bruce Bawer
While Europe Slept: How Radical Islam Is Destroying the West from Within. New York: Broadway, 2006.

Benazir Bhutto
Reconciliation: Islam, Democracy, and the West. New York: Harper, 2008.

Jarret Brachman
Global Jihadism: Theory and Practice. New York: Routledge, 2009.

Daniel Byman
The Five Front War: The Better Way to Fight Global Jihad. Hoboken, NJ: John Wiley & Sons, 2008.

John Calvert — *Islamism: A Documentary and Reference Guide*. Westport, CT: Greenwood, 2008.

Jocelynne Cesari — *When Islam and Democracy Meet: Muslims in Europe and in the United States*. New York: Palgrave Macmillan, 2006.

David Cook — *Martyrdom in Islam*. New York: Cambridge University Press, 2007.

Katerina Dalacoura — *Islam, Liberalism and Human Rights: Implications for International Relations*. London: I.B. Tauris, 2007.

Meghnad Desai — *Rethinking Islamism: The Ideology of the New Terror*. New York: I.B. Tauris, 2007.

Asghar Ali Engineer — *The Rights of Women in Islam*. New York: New Dawn, 2004.

John L. Esposito and Dalia Mogahed — *Who Speaks for Islam?: What a Billion Muslims Really Think*. New York: Gallup, 2007.

Brigitte Gabriel — *They Must Be Stopped: Why We Must Defeat Radical Islam and How We Can Do It*. New York: St. Martin's, 2008.

Peter Gottshalk and Gabriel Greenberg — *Islamophobia: Making Muslims the Enemy*. Lanham, MD: Rowman & Littlefield, 2008.

Hamid Hadji Haidar — *Liberalism and Islam: Practical Reconciliation between the Liberal State and Shiite Muslims.* New York: Palgrave Macmillan, 2008.

Jennifer Heath — *The Scimitar and the Veil: Extraordinary Women of Islam.* Mahwah, NJ: Hidden Spring, 2004.

John W. Jandora — *States without Citizens: Understanding the Islamic Crisis.* Westport, CT: Praeger Security International, 2008.

Bernard Lewis — *Islam and the West.* New York: Oxford University Press, 1993.

——— — *The Crisis of Islam: Holy War and Unholy Terror.* New York: Modern Library, 2003.

Michael J. Mazarr — *Unmodern Men in the Modern World: Radical Islam, Terrorism, and the War on Modernity.* New York: Cambridge University Press, 2007.

Brigitte L. Nacos and Oscar Torres-Reyna — *Fueling Our Fears: Stereotyping, Media Coverage, and Public Opinion of Muslim Americans.* Lanham, MD: Rowman & Littlefield, 2007.

Walid Phares — *The Confrontation: Winning the War against Future Jihad.* New York: Palgrave Macmillan, 2008.

Anne Sofie Roald — *Women in Islam: The Western Experience.* New York: Routledge, 2001.

Ziauddin Sardar and Merryl Wyn Davies	*The No-Nonsense Guide to Islam.* Oxford: New Internationalist, 2007.
Ahmed E. Souaiaia	*Contesting Justice: Women, Islam, Law, and Society.* Albany, NY: State University of New York Press, 2008.
Mohammad Ali Syed	*The Position of Women in Islam: A Progressive View.* Albany, NY: State University of New York Press, 2004.
Aaron Tyler	*Islam, the West, and Tolerance: Conceiving Coexistence.* New York: Palgrave Macmillan, 2008.
Amina Wadud	*Inside the Gender Jihad: Women's Reform in Islam.* Oxford: Oneworld, 2006.
Paul L. Williams	*The Day of Islam: The Annihilation of America and the Western World.* Amherst, NY: Prometheus, 2007.

Index